Baby Killer Christina Riggs An Anthology of True Crime

Diane Ullmer

Published by Trellis Publishing, 2021.

BABY KILLER CHRISTINA RIGGS AN ANTHOLOGY OF TRUE CRIME

First edition. July 8, 2021.

Copyright © 2021 Diane Ullmer.

ISBN: 979-8224753550

Written by Diane Ullmer.

BABY KILLER : THE TRUE STORY OF CHRISTINA MARIE RIGGS

DIANE ULLMER

Christina Riggs had all the drugs she needed.

She had filled her prescription for the anti-depressant Elavil at the pharmacy. She had stolen morphine and potassium chloride from the hospital. Now all she had to do was follow through.

"Kids," she bellowed out from the living room table. "Vitamins!"

The two sleepy-eyed children emerged from their bedroom. Christina gave them a small amount of Elavil, dropping the pill in their mouth and watching them drink it down with a cup of water.

A few minutes later, she carried them both back to bed.

Looking down at her two young children, she began to sob.

Shelby, just two years old, in her pink jumper. Justin, five years old, in his white pajamas with battleship designs.

I have to do this. Things will only get worse for them.

THE GREATEST TABOO

Christina Marie Riggs was twenty-six years when she decided to kill her children.

"A mother is supposed to protect her own children," Riggs' Defense Attorney John Wesley Hall Jr. said. "And here she didn't and it doesn't make sense. Two defenseless children that didn't know what was coming."

After Christina sedated her children, she proceeded with her plan of injecting them with potassium chloride. She knew that the drug was administered for lethal injection executions and would stop the heart within minutes.

What she didn't know was that the drug had to be administered in a diluted form. If it is injected without any dilution, it will burn through the skin then burst through the vein.

Ignorant of the consequences, Christina injected the lethal cocktail into her son Justin first.

She wanted a painless death. She did not want her children to go through life suffering like she did.

But then her son woke up screaming.

The potassium chloride she injected was binding and burning through his blood vessel linings.

He cried and cried and wouldn't stop.

Christina began crying herself...

CHILDHOOD TRAUMA

Christina Riggs had a troubled childhood growing up in Oklahoma City, OK.

She was separated from her brothers and sisters after her parent's divorce. Raised alone by her mother, she detailed in a prison diary sexual abuses that took place in her childhood.

She wrote how her stepbrother sexually abusing her from the age of seven to thirteen. At the age of thirteen, she was molested by a neighbor as well.

By the time she entered her teenage years, Christina was obese, using food as an emotional outlet. She also began abusing alcohol and marijuana.

"She indulged in overeating because she didn't want to appear attractive," forensic psychologist Paula Orange said. "That behavior was part of a psychological response to being molested. 'If I become fat and ugly then he won't want me anymore.' No one will bother me, no one will hurt me."

In her teenage years, however, Christina began to use sex as a way to get what she wanted, which was love.

"It isn't uncommon for abused young women to become very promiscuous," Orange said. "It is learned behavior. She became defective, if you will, and should have gotten help. Unfortunately, this is not a good recipe for someone who wants to have a healthy stable relationship and raise children."

"I felt that no boy liked me because of my weight," Christina wrote in her journal. "So I became sexually promiscuous because I thought that was the only way I could have a boyfriend."

She became pregnant by the age of sixteen but gave the baby boy up for adoption.

After high school, Christina went to a vocational school to become a licensed practical nurse (LPN). She obtained employment as a home care nurse and then later worked full-time at a VA hospital.

Her dating life remained steady albeit unsuccessful. She went from one man to the next, dating a Navy ensign named Jon Riggs and a bouncer before meeting Timothy Thompson. Thompson was an Air Force private at Tinker Air Force Base.

Three years after her first child, Christina would become pregnant with Timothy's baby. She informed Timothy her pregnancy the day before he was to be discharged from the Air Force.

Timothy, however, did not take the news well. He would not accept responsibility and moved back to his native Minnesota.

"Chrissy's luck with men was about zero to nothing," Carol Thomas, Christina's mother said.

But while her relationship ended with Timothy, Christina hooked back up with Jon Riggs who returned home after being on leave with the Navy.

"It was great," Christina wrote. "He felt the baby's first kick. As far as he was concerned, it was his baby."

Justin Thomas was born on June 7th, 1992.

"As I held Justin in my arms and looked into his little face, I became so scared," Christina wrote. "Would I be a good Mom? Could I give him all he needed?"

Riggs would move in with Christina and the two hoped for the best. Christina would become pregnant again and the couple would marry in July of 1993.

But misfortune would strike again as Christina would suffer a miscarriage on her wedding night.

The marriage would go south from there as Christina alternated between being depressed to having suicidal thoughts. She blamed her mental state on her birth control medication and a doctor gave her the anti-depressant Prozac.

The medication worked for a while but then Christina inexplicably stopped taking the drug. She kept her sadness to herself and didn't want to burden others with her problems.

"She's always been that way," Christina's mother said. "If I pushed her hard she might get mad and tell me what was going on."

By 1994, Christina would become pregnant and deliver a healthy baby girl in December named Shelby. This would mark the high point of Christina's life as "Sissie" and "Bubbie", the two nicknames for her children, brought immeasurable joy into her life.

She would write that it was the happiest time of her life as both she and Jon cried when they held their new baby in their arms. Things were happy for once in her life.

Christina continued to work as a vocational nurse and was assigned to work at a triage station which served to help the victims of the Oklahoma City Federal Building terrorist bombing. She would suffer post-traumatic stress disorder as a result. Later at her trial, the prosecuting attorneys would argue that the hospital had no record of Christina serving after the bombing. This may be nitpicking as authorities were lenient with record keeping during that urgent situation.

STRESS AND STRAIN

A year later, the couple would move to Sherwood, Arkansas to be closer to Christina's mother, Carole.

Carole worked as a food service worker at Baptist Hospital and Christina was able to find a job there as well, once again working as a licensed practical nurse.

The children go on to have ailments that would stress out the already fragile Christina. Shelby would have chronic ear infections that made doctor visits a routine thing. Justin was diagnosed with attention deficit disorder and his hyper nature would grate on the nerves of his parents.

Financial difficulties and the stress of running a family would put a strain on the marriage and the couple would eventually divorce. Her husband, Jon Riggs, had a volatile temper that he eventually took out on the young Justin. Jon would punch Justin in the abdomen with such force that the young boy had to go to the emergency room.

Jon would then abandon the family.

"Justin would say, 'My Daddy hurt me, and then he went away,' " Christina's mother recalled.

Christina would receive limited child support from Jon and had to work long hours to provide for her family. The more hours she worked, the more she had to pay for daycare which proved to be a daily traumatic event.

Shelby would cry as Christina would leave her at the facility.

"She was beating on the glass, yelling, 'Mama! Mama!' " Christina recalled.

Despite her increased efforts, Christina could not get ahead financially. She began writing bad checks. Bills remained unpaid. Car insurance. Car registration. Lights and utilities.

"I started out in a boat with a small hole," Christina said. "But the hole kept getting bigger, and no matter how hard you bail, you keep sinking. I was tired and I gave up. Suicide seemed like the only thing."

A HISTORY OF MENTAL ILLNESS

Christina had a cousin that killed herself. Her mother had also tried to kill herself when Christina was a baby. Her grandmother was committed to a mental institution.

But Christina would outdo them all in one fateful night.

"Just speaking in general," Orange said. "When mothers kill their children they do not poison them. In the case of Christina, she was applying what she thought would be a lethal injection."

But even with a history of mental illness in the family, nobody could have predicted how the sweet and caring Christina could commit such a heinous crime.

"Chrissy always wanted to help people," Christina's sister, Elizabeth Nottingham said. "She was always helping someone."

But Nottingham had some valuable psychological insight on her sister. She was a mental health counselor and had been close to Christina.

She wanted to know what drove her sister to kill her own children. After her sister's arrest, she began fishing around her house, looking for some kind of clue, a sign that everyone had missed.

"I was almost hoping to find that she wasn't a good parent," Nottingham said. "Then I could be mad at her. You know, I went through her house with a fine toothed comb. All the chemicals were locked away. The food was in the refrigerator. Even pictures of their fathers was in their room above each of their beds. She was great with the kids."

MORE TROUBLE WITH MEN

What Christina's sister would find out was that she simply could not find a decent man. That one relationship where everything would be ideal.

After her divorce from Jon, Christina would enter into another relationship which again would not go well.

"The guy didn't just break her heart," Nottingham said. "But took her credit card. I mean, it's one thing to have someone dump you, it's another to have someone rip you off and leave you destitute too."

After this break-up, Christina would sit at her dining room table both broke and broken-hearted. She had no man in her life. She had no means to pay her family's bills.

Seeing only dark lights ahead, Christina would lapse into a deep depression. She went to her doctor again who prescribed her more Prozac which used irregularly.

"She may have stopped taking the Prozac when she killed the babies," Orange said. "When someone just stops that medication cold-turkey it can have some side effects like increased irritability, irrational mood changes, and an even deeper depression."

"So she had the perfect storm brewing," Nottingham said. "She had depression, she had all of these personal failures. You know, people talk about having rainy days and Mondays. And in fact 'Rainy days and Mondays' was the CD that was in her CD player."

BACK TO THAT FATEFUL NIGHT

Christina had to kill herself. Her emotional bank account had been overdrawn for years.

But she couldn't stand the thought of leaving her children alone.

"If she left the kids behind," Hall Jnr said. "She was afraid that the children would be separated, go to their father's, for instance, and be split up."

"She just thought there was no other way out," Nottingham said. "She thought that no one else would take care of her kids. And that they would be better off, in her mind, she was saving them from future sadness."

With Justin screaming in pain, Christina panicked. She began sobbing but whatever remain of her maternal instinct kicked in and she tried to inject him with morphine.

Toxicology reports didn't reveal whether or not she did this.

But what she did do was suffocate her young son with a pillow. Sobbing, she then did the same deed to her baby daughter, Shelby.

Shaking with adrenaline and grief, Christina wobbled on shaky legs back to her living room. She took out her bottle of Elavil, an anti-depressant, and swallowed the remaining twenty-eight pills. Her nerves calming, she tried injecting the potassium chloride into her own arm.

The chemical burn right through her vein, collapsing it.

The drugs began taking effect and Christina fainted to the floor, hoping her nightmare would finally end.

THE DAY AFTER

The lethal mixture had burned a half-inch hole into Christina's arm. She didn't show up for work the next day and her mother called her cell phone and land line repeatedly.

Worried that she received no response, Carole drove to Christina's apartment and let herself in.

To her horror, she thought everyone was dead, including Christina.

"All I could do was turn around and around and scream and holler, 'No. No. No.' There's no way to describe how I felt."

Frantic, she called 911 and yelling into the phone, "My daughter and babies are dead."

Paramedics would arrive.

The children were dead.

But the medics were able to resuscitate Christina. She was transported to the intensive care unit and was kept under guard by the police.

"I had to do it so I wouldn't leave them behind," Christina was overheard saying in her hospital room. The treating physician, Dr. Jim Rice, would later testify that Christina as "combative at times" and "just incoherent and not really making any sense."

As soon as Christina became reasonably coherent, she was taken to the police station for booking.

THE INTERROGATION

On November 6th, 1997, Christina was interrogated by a Detective Jones and Detective Sharon Williams.

"Christina, what we are doing is investigating the death of your two babies. Do you want to tell us what happened?" Jones asked.

"I killed them," Christina said, crying.

"What did you say?"

"I said-"

"Did you say you killed them?"

"I'm sorry."

"How did you go about doing that?" Jones asked.

"I got some bottles and stuff from here...I need a cigarette...Darvocet."

"Are you saying that you got some medicine from the hospital?"

Christina nodded.

"Christina, how did you do it? Did you give them an injection? Did you give them a shot?"

"I tried to ... and ... I did it with Justin because I figured with him being the oldest one that he would give me more problems. So, I tried it with him and I thought it would just stop his heart. But it hurt. Oh, he said it hurt ...It didn't work, he just kept calling, 'Momma! Momma! Momma!' I just figured it was too late now because I had no place to turn back to. I cleaned out my checking account and gave my mother all the money I had."

"Christina, why did you do this?" Jones asked.

"Because I wanted to die," Christina said, crying again. "But I didn't want to die and leave my kids behind or for them to be a burden to somebody else. I didn't want them to think I didn't love them and I didn't want them to grow up separately because they have two different Daddies. And I knew if I passed away they would be fighting my Mother for custody and I didn't want that for nobody."

"You felt like you were doing it for the kids' sake?"

"In a way, yeah... my piece of mind."

"Christina, did you really want to die?"

Christina didn't respond. She continued crying.

"And you felt it would be better if your children just die with you and ... were the children already dead before you took your medicine?"

"Yes."

"How long had they been dead before you took your medicine?"

"About twenty minutes."

"About twenty minutes?"

"That's because I drank and got up and smoked a cigarette and got back and sit for a minute and...I was like, 'Okay, I'm going to do it now. I can't turn back now because you've already killed Justin.' And ... so I did it."

"What time did you give them the medicine? Do you remember?"

"Justin about 10:15 or 10:30."

"10:15 or 10:30 in the morning?"

"No, in the evening."

"Oh, in the evening?"

"Last night."

"Okay."

"Then I smoked another cigarette and waited," Christina paused. "And suffocated Shelby."

"You suffocated Shelby? What did ... how did you suffocate her?"

"I put a pillow over her head."

"Okay, Did you ... Had you given her any medicine at all, or ... any of the Morphine or the Potassium Chloride?"

"I slipped them ... I made them drink half of an Elavil because I figured that would make them sleep a little bit better so that it wouldn't wake them."

"So, Shelby, you killed her with a pillow. You suffocated her. And what about the little boy. How did you do him?"

"I gave him the medicine and when it didn't work."

"You suffocated him too?"

"Yes."

"With a pillow? Were they fighting while you suffocated them?"

"Justin did. Shelby a little bit but not much," Christina began to cry again.

"When did you decide to do this, Christina? On what day did you decide to do this?"

"Uh ... the best I remember it was Sunday night or Saturday night because we was out talking and this and that and the other ... and they caught me."

"Who caught you?"

"I was depressed. I was thinking about what was going on in my life and that things aren't always working for me and..."

"When did you get those drugs from the hospital?"

"When? Yesterday."

"Yesterday? You mean the day that you killed them? Is that the day that you got the drugs? The last was it ... "

"Was it the last day that you worked at the hospital or the day before that? "I think ..."

"When you got ... "

"I got the drugs and I gave them to my kids. That's the only drugs that I had in my hand. And I know that there was three Valiums in a vial in there, but there wasn't enough to even cover the jar up and put it in my pocket and bring them home. And I know I should have thought better ... had somebody rinsing with me, but ... they were just what came home in my pockets."

"Did you know what you were going to do when you took the drugs from the hospital? Did you have intentions of giving them to your children? And how many days did you think about this before you killed your children?"

"About three weeks. Two weeks."

"Two or three weeks. In other words, you've been thinking about doing this for the last two or three weeks? What made you decide to just go ahead and do it?"

"I just can't take it no more."

"You couldn't take it anymore."

"I felt like I was out of control," Christina said.

"Did you just feel like your life was in a mess? Had you talked to anybody about this? Your Mom or anybody?"

"I've tried to talk to people about what I feel and what I think and they were just like, 'I don't have time right now. We'll do it some other time.' So, I just got to where I don't care anymore. I tried but they can't give me no help."

"So you just felt like nobody was listening to you? Okay, Christina ...Christina, do you have anything more to say about your babies or anything? "I wish I hadn't done it now."

Christina would then go on an incoherent ramble, explaining how she saw her mother riding down an escalator with a bunch of old people. The detectives, however, got the damning evidence they needed and ended the interrogation.

PRISON AND JAIL

Christina would find a hostile environment in prison. The majority of her fellow prisoners were women who were taken away from their children by force. They had contempt for Christina's crime.

One inmate spat in her face and her life was threatened.

Christina was then moved to an isolated cell where she remained until her trial.

She would be charged with two counts of first-degree murder which was punishable by death in the state of Arkansas.

"We tried to show that she was under extreme emotional disturbance," Hall Jr said. "To justify either not imposing the death penalty or hopefully finding her guilty of second-degree murder."

"I just hope that out of all her misery," Nottingham said. "The sadness of our family. That we can shed some light on the causes of this for other people and that maybe they'll be able to look at the symptoms and look at the situations and maybe intervene for someone else."

But the prosecuting attorney, as well as the community, believed that Christina was guilty of performing a selfish act, an act wherein she tried to free herself from motherhood.

The most damning evidence at the trial, aside from the interrogation tapes, would be the account of the physicians.

One doctor would testify that it would take three to six minutes to suffocate someone to death. Because of that time period, the jurors would be able to envision how Christina commit a willful act of murder. Christina had, in essence, a struggling toddler under her pillow for about three to six minutes...suffocating to death.

"They just wanted her to be evil," Nottingham said of the prosecuting attorney's intent. "It was easier that way."

"Essentially, what the jury saw was that she was self-centered," argued Pulaski Prosecuting Attorney Larry Jegley. "That she viewed the children as an inconvenience and an interference with what she wanted to pursue. She placed her interests above those of the children."

Jegley argued that Christina was a self-centered and premeditated murderer. He brought up the fact that she had locked the children up in the house (according to a neighbor) in order that she could go out to a Karaoke party. He urged the jury not to buy into her manipulation to feel sorry for her. "There were lots of people who have it worse than she did."

The jury would side with the prosecution and find Christina guilty after a very short deliberation period.

THE IRONY

Christina Riggs would be sentenced to death by lethal injection via potassium chloride...The same method that she used to try to kill her children and herself.

"It was a cruel irony that they finished what she started," Hall Jr said. "Almost the exact same way except she was strapped down to a table."

Christina would appeal the sentencing but did so with reluctance. She wanted to die.

"I'll be with my children and with God," Christina said. "I'll be where there's no more pain. Maybe I'll find some peace."

Her defense attorney John Wesley Hall Jr was allowed to witness the execution.

"You can see their face," Hall Jr said. "It allows them to say their last words. The face changes color as the drugs take effect. You turn gray. The skin turns gray. And it's rather shocking to watch it happen."

"She was so depressed that it became this black sheet over her eyes that she couldn't see through," Orange said. "She wanted to spare her own children from the kind of life that she had. She had lost complete hope and really over thought things. That's how her depression warped her. It warped her enough to think that she was doing her children a favor by killing them."

Christina was sent to death row and was haunted by the memories of her children. She openly stated that she tried "not to think about them" because when she did it was like someone "ripping them away from her all over again."

"A lot of regret," Christina said. "That's what goes through my mind, day-in, day-out. God's punishing me. He let me live so I would suffer."

Riggs was flown in from McPherson Jail to Cummins in order to prep for her execution. She would be administered the lethal injection at 9:28 PM CDT on May 2nd, 2000.

"No words can express just how sorry I am for taking the lives of my babies," Riggs said in a prepared statement. "No way I can make up for or take away the pain I have caused everyone who knew and loved them. I love you, my babies."

CHRISTA PIKE

Christa Gail Pike, born 10 March 1976, currently sits on Tennessee's death row for the murder of Colleen Slemmer, 19, on 12 January 1995. The murder occurred when Pike was 18 years old. Pike and her then-boyfriend Tadaryl Shipp who was 17 at the time of the murder were convicted of Slemmer's murder and conspiracy to commit murder. Another friend of the defendants and the victim, Shadolla Peterson, also 18 at the time, was convicted as an accessory after the fact and given six years' probation after turning informant. Pike was sentenced to death by electrocution in 1996 and, at the time, she had the distinction of being the youngest woman ever to be sentenced to death, in any state and only the second women given the death penalty in Tennessee.

Early Life

Pike's life reads like a primer for depraved murderers. As a small child, Pike did not enjoy a healthy and supportive bond with her mother, Carissa Hansen, a licensed nurse, allegedly because of her premature birth. Whereas thousands of children are born prematurely and do not resort to criminal behavior Pike's birth was presented as evidence of one possible origin of her poor and troubled behavior. Pike's maternal grandmother was verbally abusive and Pike was raised by her alcoholic and abusive paternal grandmother until the latter's death in 1988 when Pike was 12; after which Pike attempted suicide by overdosing. She was then shuttled back and forth between her divorced parents' homes. In 1989, Pike was kicked out of her father's house for the second and final time due to her unruliness and the alleged sexual abuse of her father's then-two-year old daughter with his second wife.

Prior to the murder, experts assert that there were myriad indications that Pike was seriously disturbed; however, nobody who may have suspected this sought help for the increasingly disobedient and incorrigible young lady. According to Pike's mother, she was problematic since the age of eight and the two of them had a contentious relationship due to Pike's fluctuating and troubling behavior. Her mother asserted that by age nine Pike was growing marijuana in pots at their home and had been permitted to have a live-in boyfriend at age 14. At one point—in an effort to improve their relationship—Hansen suggested that she and Pike smoke marijuana together. Hansen mistakenly believed that cultivating a friendship with her daughter would cultivate the necessary bond Pike had been lacking her entire life. At one point, one of her mother's boyfriends whipped Pike with a belt which prompted her to wield a butcher knife against him before he was subsequently arrested. Hansen also admitted that Pike had repeatedly lied to and stolen from her. In several interviews with Hansen throughout Pike's trial and seemingly endless appeals, she admitted repeatedly that she was a terrible mother and should have spent more time with her daughter.

Pike's aunt, Carrie Ross, provided insight into Pike's upbringing when she testified that she disallowed her own children from associating with Pike because she lived in a filthy house that had zero ground rules and that Pike was a pathological liar of whom she was somewhat afraid. She also admitted that there was a history of substance abuse in Pike's family. Ross also stated that on the few occasions that Pike actually visited her she behaved like a little girl and engaged in Barbie and dress-up play with her eleven-year-old cousin. Further, there were some allegations that Pike may have been sexually abused but these were neither confirmed nor denied.

Pike's father, Glenn Pike testified that he did, in fact, kick his daughter out of his house multiple times; the last time being in 1989 after the aforementioned allegations that Pike sexually abused her two-year old half-sister. He admitted that he had signed adoption papers for Pike prior to her 18th birthday and that during the times she resided with him she was manipulative, disobedient, and dishonest.

After dropping out of high school, Pike began Job Corps classes in computer programming. Job Corps is a government-based organization that provides occupational and vocational training to underprivileged and troubled teens. It was at the now-defunct Job Corps center in Knoxville where she met Shipp, Slemmer, and Peterson. While Job Corps seeks to promote prosocial behavior and foster a strong desire among its participants to learn a vocation and secure a more promising future than might have been previously the case, this program is also known to cultivate criminal activity, likely due to the association among its participants; many of whom already had problematic behavior.

Evidence of Premeditation

On 11 January 1995, the day before the actual homicide, Pike told friend and co-Job Corps student Kim Iloilo that she was planning to kill Slemmer because she "just felt mean that day." Iloilo discounted Pike's statement as nothing more than merely talk; however, the following evening at approximately 8:00 p.m. Iloilo witnessed Pike, Shipp, Peterson, and Slemmer leaving the Job Corps center. When Iloilo saw Pike, Shipp, and Peterson returning at approximately 10:15 p.m. without Slemmer she, again, thought nothing of it. Even when Pike visited Iloilo's dorm room at 11:00 p.m. that night and confessed to killing Slemmer—as well as showing Iloilo what Pike identified as a piece of Slemmer's skull—Iloilo still failed to tell anyone. Later, at Pike's trial, Iloilo testified that while Pike was iterating the events of the murder she was oddly smiling, singing, and dancing around the room. The following morning Iloilo asked Pike what she was going to do with the piece of skull. Pike nonchalantly replied that she had it in her pocket and was, in fact, eating breakfast with it.

Pike also told another student, Stephanie Wilson, a similar account the following day and proudly described the brown spots on her shoes as blood. Not unlike Iloilo, Wilson failed to immediately report anything.

The Crime Scene

On 13 January, officers from the University of Tennessee and Knoxville Police Departments were dispatched to greenhouses on the University's agricultural campus in Tyson Park where a University grounds department employee reported finding, at approximately 8:05 a.m., what he assumed to be a dead animal. The gruesome discovery was a corpse that turned out to be Colleen Slemmer. She was naked from the waist up; her throat was cut; her head had been bludgeoned; and she had various cuts all over her arms, throat, and torso—including a pentagram that had been carved into her chest. Officer John Terry Johnson who testified at Pike's trial described Slemmer's body as so badly beaten that she was unrecognizable as a human being. He also stated that he thought he was looking at her face when, in reality,

Slemmer was lying face-down in the dirt and debris where Pike, Shipp, and Peterson had left her.

There was additional evidence and testimony that the crime scene encompassed an area that measured 100 feet long by 60 feet wide; an astounding 6,000 square feet in area. Despite the area being muddy and wet there was ample evidence of a physical struggle with trampled bushes, a considerable amount of blood, body drag marks, and hand and knee prints. Thirty feet from Slemmer's body was a large pool of blood which suggested that Slemmer was attacked in one area and then dragged to where her body was later found. Slemmer's shirt and bra were also discovered at the crime scene, as well as a bloody rag that Pike admitted to tying over Slemmer's mouth at one point to keep her from screaming.

Disturbingly, University of Tennessee police officer Harold James Underwood, Jr., who was the officer assigned to secure the crime scene, testified at trial that Pike and a few other females came to the scene between four and five p.m. the day of the discovery and before Pike was even considered to be a suspect. Underwood stated that Pike had asked why the wooded area was marked off, who the victim was, and whether police had any leads as to who the suspect or suspects were. He particularly recalled Pike's odd behavior—moving around a lot while giggling amusedly—and that she wore a necklace in the shape of a pentagram. The following day, during briefing when informed that the victim had a pentagram carved into her chest, Underwood reported Pike's behavior and necklace to his supervisors.

Autopsy and Findings

During Slemmer's autopsy, the medical examiner, Dr. Sandra Elkins, had to identify the victim's body from dental records because her head was so bludgeoned that she was unrecognizable. After cleaning up Slemmer's body which was clad only in jeans, socks, and shoes, and covered with dirt and twigs, Dr. Elkins began cataloging Slemmer's wounds. Due to the sheer number of wounds on her back, arms, abdomen, and chest, and the fact that following department policy which stated that each individual wound be assigned a letter of the alphabet, when Dr. Elkins reached double letters she, instead, individually catalogued only the most serious wounds and that there were innumerable other superficial and defensive wounds. Among the most serious cuts was a six-inch gaping wound across Slemmer's throat that was deep enough to penetrate the fat and muscles in her neck as well as the aforementioned pentagram. Additional injuries included fresh bruising which Dr. Elkins asserted was consistent with crawling.

Cause of death was ultimately attributed to blunt force trauma to the head. Dr. Elkins surmised that Slemmer's head was hit with the asphalt at least four times—two to the left side, one over the right eye, and one to the nose—which collectively resulted in multiple and extensive skull fractures. One of these blows was to the left side of Slemmer's head—which, according to Dr. Elkins, occurred with the right side of the victim's head against a firm surface. This blow only fractured her skull but also imbedded a portion of Slemmer's skull into her head and contained black particles from the piece of asphalt determined to be the murder weapon.

Even more tragic was Dr. Elkins' findings that none of Slemmer's other wounds would have rendered her unconscious and evidence of active blood flow around the wounds and blood in her sinus cavity indicated that Slemmer was alive during the severe torture she suffered before being killed.

Arrest and Confession

The police quickly connected Pike to the homicide thanks to the piece of Slemmer's skull discovered in Pike's jacket pocket. Pike had left this jacket hanging on the back of a chair in Job Corps Orientation Specialist Robert A. Pollock's office on 13 January after meeting with him about a misplaced ID card. Pike's jacket remained in Pollock's office from 4:00 p.m. on 13 January until 7:30 a.m. on 17 January. After learning over the weekend that Pike was a suspect in Slemmer's murder investigation, Pollock immediately gave the jacket to William Hudson, the Job Corps' safety and security captain who turned it over to Knoxville Police Department Officer Arthur Bohanan. At trial, Bohanan would testify that he found a small piece of bone in one of the pockets and presented it to Dr. Murray Marks, a University of Tennessee forensic anthropologist who was reconstructing Slemmer's decapitated skull and the piece in Pike's jacket pocket fit perfectly into an area where a portion of her skull was missing at the time of the victim's discovery.

When confronted with this evidence and subsequently arrested, Pike waived her *Miranda* protections and confessed to the murder and permitted officers to search her dorm room where the blood-soaked jeans she wore the previous night were found. Additionally, Pike led officers to a trash can at a nearby Texaco station on Cumberland Avenue where she had disposed of Slemmer's ID and a pair of gloves Pike had been wearing at the time of the homicide.

Pike's transcribed confession was 46 pages long.

In it, Pike admitted that there was animosity between Slemmer and her because Pike was convinced that Slemmer was a rival for the affections of her boyfriend, Shipp, and that Slemmer was trying to get Pike kicked out of the Job Corps program so she could have Shipp for herself. Pike also claimed that she had awakened one night to find Slemmer standing above her with a box cutter; however, there is no evidence of this allegation. Instead, Slemmer had repeatedly called her mother, May Martinez, to tell her she was afraid of Pike who she had awakened to find in her room and that she wanted to come home; to which Slemmer's mother said that she couldn't because she had signed a contract. Pike stated that she had only planned to fight Slemmer to stop her from running her mouth. On that fateful night of 12 January, Pike, Slemmer, Shipp, and Peterson signed the Job Corps logbook as they were leaving for an outing Slemmer believed was to smoke marijuana en route to a video store so that Pike and she could try to work out their problems.

When the group entered a tunnel at the edge of Tyson Park, Slemmer likely felt that something was not quite right and proceeded to ask Pike where they were going and whether there was, in fact, any marijuana. These questions irritated Pike who began the brutal assault shortly thereafter after they had gone deeply enough into the woods so that nobody could hear them that led to Slemmer's murder.

Pike confessed to initially slamming Slemmer's head into her knee and then throwing her to the ground where Pike continually punched, kicked, and slammed Slemmer's head into the concrete, screaming, "the bi*ch won't die" and that she wanted "to see [Slemmer's] brains flow." According to witnesses Shipp and Peterson, as Slemmer continued to plead with Pike to stop, Pike got angrier and more brutal. Slemmer offered to return to her Florida home, leave her belongings at the Job Corps center, and not tell anyone what happened; however, Pike became more enraged and yelled at Slemmer to be quiet because "it was harder to hurt someone who was talking to you."

In addition to the savage beating, Slemmer had been cut innumerable times with a box cutter and a mini meat cleaver (that Pike had allegedly borrowed from another Job Corps student) to her torso, arms, face, and back including having had her throat slit six times prior to the fatal blow that resulted from having her head crushed by a piece of asphalt. There was also a pentagram carved into Slemmer's chest; however, Pike asserted that Shipp had done that. Pike also confessed to "just watching Slemmer bleed" when the victim got up and tried to run away. Pike admitted to cutting Slemmer's back: "the big long cut."

After the murder, Pike stated that she and Shipp washed their hands and shoes in a nearby mud puddle to conceal the blood, dumped the box cutter, and Pike returned the meat cleaver to the person from which she borrowed it. This person has never been identified.

The physical evidence and co-defendant testimony suggested that the assault and murder lasted from 30 minutes to an hour and consisted of Slemmer repeatedly trying to get up and run away but was prevented from doing so by the co-defendants who also, as Pike testified, contributed to the physical assault by throwing rocks at Slemmer's head and holding her down so she couldn't run away. Later, Pike would testify that she heard voices in her head overriding Slemmer's continual screaming, telling her that she needed to prevent Slemmer from filing charges against her for attempted murder. Pike also admitted that at one point she thought she had heard a noise and went to investigate it to ensure that they were alone, as well as alleging that during the assault she heard Slemmer breathing in blood and jerking but did not let this assuage her anger as Pike continued her savagery.

Even more troublesome, a police video recorded after Pike's confession shows Pike smiling and providing extensive details about the crime at the crime scene, oftentimes mimicking her actions that evening. Many have said that her demeanor on the recording was eerily similar to that of a little girl who was excited and happy that she had experienced the best day of her life and had no problem talking about the events that transpired, the heinousness of her actions, and how she felt about it all.

The facts of the homicide are not nor have they ever been in dispute, thanks to an abundance of evidence. Pike's confession, and witness testimony at the trial.

Pre-Trial Examination

Prior to her trial, Pike was given a battery of assessment tests and examined by numerous psychiatrists including clinical psychologist Dr. Eric Engum who found her to be extremely bright as evidenced by an I.Q. of 111—in the 77th percentile of the general population—which he believed to be remarkable given her difficult childhood and lack of formal schooling beyond the ninth grade. Dr. Engum also found that

Pike had excellent reasoning, problem solving, language, and analytic skills, and was also quite adept at paying attention, sustaining concentration, and sequencing information. Dr. Engum concluded that Pike was legally sane and had no brain damage which has frequently been demonstrated to cause violent behavior in some individuals.

Of particular interest was that Pike was found to be marijuana- and inhalant-dependent and also diagnosed with borderline personality disorder. Whereas there are some similarities between borderline personality disorder and antisocial personality disorder such as impulsivity, irritability, aggression, and a self-image that fluctuates between self-aggrandizement and despair, there are several differences. Individuals with borderline personality disorder differ from those with antisocial behavior in that the former—which primarily affects females—is characterized by a lack of remorse, self-destructiveness, black-and-white thinking, alcohol and/or drug use or abuse, unstable relationships characterized by fear of abandonment and extreme swings between love and hate, difficulty in achieving academic and vocational goals, and are more likely to have been sexually abused; while the latter—which affects disproportionately more males—is characterized by a lack of affect and remorse, emptiness, and an ultimate goal of self-preservation.

Pike demonstrated all of the aforementioned characteristics of borderline personality disorder which makes it easier—but not justifiably so—to comprehend how her intense jealousy of Slemmer and fear of losing Shipp made her commit her atrocious acts. In addition to her fear of abandonment, Pike also abused drugs, was likely sexually abused, had contentious relationships, and displayed zero remorse. Dr. Engum surmised that Pike did not act with premeditation or deliberation in Slemmer's murder but, instead, in a manner that was consistent with borderline personality disorder. More simply, Pike had lost control. However, on cross-examination Dr. Engum admitted that Pike's deliberate luring of Slemmer, that she carved a pentagram in the victim's chest, that she brought weapons with her, and that she bashed Slemmer's head into the concrete does, in fact, constitute deliberateness.

That Pike was overjoyed and singing in Iloilo's room describing the murder while dancing around with the portion of Slemmer's skull Pike had taken as a trophy further supported Dr. Engum's diagnosis of borderline personality disorder because she had eliminated who she perceived was in competition for her boyfriend, Shipp, and, therefore, could continue her relationship with him. When questioned about the piece of skull Pike had taken, Dr. Engum said that Pike had no identity and her actions of taking and displaying the skull was a way to get recognition, no matter how misleading and distorted said recognition might be. In fact, after her conviction and sentencing Pike wrote a letter to Shipp which was intercepted by jail personnel that stated that even though she tried to be "nice" to Slemmer by bashing in her head instead of letting her bleed to death she was still sentenced to "fry."

The Trial

There was an abundance of evidence presented at the trial. Physical evidence consisted of crime scene photographs, autopsy reports, bloody clothing, and the piece of Slemmer's skull Pike had taken as a trophy. With respect to this skull piece, Dr. Elkins presented Slemmer's decapitated skull that was reconstructed by Dr. Marks to explain the victim's injuries. The skull presented at trial was complete except for a portion that was missing on the left side of Slemmer's skull. Dr. Elkins demonstrated that the piece of skull found in Pike's jacket fit perfectly into this spot, much to the chagrin of Slemmer's mother who, in a taped interview, stated that Pike was oftentimes giggling and passing notes to her mother and defense attorney during the trial, not unlike an immature middle-schooler.

At the trial, the State introduced photographs taken of Pike and Shipp at the Knoxville Police Department in which both were wearing pentagram necklaces similar to the shape carved into Slemmer's chest. It was presented that both Pike and Shipp dabbled in devil worshiping and other forms of the occult and that Slemmer was a sacrifice for the next day, Friday the 13th. Despite the presence of some type of satanic elements in Slemmer's murder, Dr. William Bernet, Vanderbilt University's psychiatric hospital medical director, testified that the evidence was that of "an adolescent dabbling in Satanism." He further concluded that the concept of collective aggression—or mob mentality—in which a group of people become stimulated and subsequently engage in some type of violent behavior was most assuredly at play in the events leading to Slemmer's death. However, Dr. Bernet ultimately stated that he did not have enough evidence to definitively surmise whether Pike had acted with premeditation or intent when she lured and murdered Slemmer.

Pike was ultimately convicted of first-degree murder and conspiracy to commit first-degree murder after a mere two-and-a-half hours of jury deliberation. The fact that the jury returned guilty verdicts for first-degree murder—and did it so quickly—demonstrate that jurors were convinced that Pike had the requisite mens rea, or mental capacity, to warrant a first-degree murder charge: premeditation and deliberation. Amidst the overwhelming evidence and utter lack of remorse for her actions Pike was sentenced to death by electrocution (Tennessee has since adopted lethal injection for executions but has the prerogative to utilize electrocution if the lethal injection drugs cannot be obtained). Shipp was sentenced to life without parole because his age at the time of the murder was too young to warrant capital punishment and Peterson turned informant and was given six years' probation for her testimony.

Pike's conviction was upheld by the Court of Criminal Appeals and the United States Supreme Court denied certiorari.

Post-Conviction

While incarcerated, Pike demonstrated more evidence of her depravity. In 2001 she tried to murder fellow inmate Patricia Jones by strangling her with a shoelace. Pike alleges that Jones repeatedly tortured her by calling her "fried chicken" and making various demeaning sounds as an affront to what Jones said was the sound that Pike would make when she was electrocuted. The final straw was when Jones physically threatened Pike's friend, fellow devil worshiper Natasha Cornet. Pike said that she jumped atop Jones and choked her with a shoelace so that the much larger and heavier Jones would get off of Cornet. By the time prison guards reached them, Jones was unconscious.

Pike was subsequently convicted of attempted murder despite her prior death sentence because any offense committed while an individual is incarcerated must be adjudicated. During this time, neurology specialist Dr. Jonathan Henry Pincus began investigating Pike's brain to glean some type of knowledge as to why Pike behaved and continued to act violently the way she did when she assaulted Jones. He asserted that every killer he has ever examined share three commonalities: brain damage, a history of abuse, and mental illness. Dr. Pincus alleged that Pike did, in fact, possess all three features and demonstrates all of the requisite features common to serial killers. There is much consensus among professionals that Pike would likely have been a serial killer had she not been caught the first time.

He also testified at Pike's attempted murder trial that her brain's frontal lobes are not "put together properly"; largely due, he claimed, to the fact that Pike's mother drank while she was pregnant with Pike despite denial of this by Pike's mother. It was also brought up that as a child Pike played at the slaughterhouse where her grandfather worked and that she was frequently subjected to pornography and horror movies on the home television screen. He asserted that all of these factors provide insight into how an 18-year old girl could act with such depravity as was the case when Pike murdered Slemmer.

However, the original trial judge, Mary Beth Leibowitz, stated that Pincus' "findings" of brain damage was curious as the defense expert at Pike's original trial who was trying to spare her the death penalty failed to find such evidence.

Forensic psychiatrist William Kenner testified that Pike had suffered from undiagnosed bipolar disorder, the symptoms of which were evident from the time Pike was a "sleepless, talkative adolescent" and likened her to an automobile with cruise control set at 120 miles per hour. Pike's post-conviction defense team alleged that this non-diagnosis justified her requesting a new trial.

In 2002 Pike sought to have her appeal legally stopped and to proceed with her execution. In June of that year Judge Leibowitz granted Pike's request and scheduled an execution date of 19 August 2002. However, a few days later Pike changed her mind and the Tennessee Court of Appeals subsequently stayed her execution. In October 2005, Pike's death sentence was affirmed; however, no execution date has been set at this time.

Pike was again in court in 2007 when her defense team headed by Donald E. Dawson asserted sought a new trial, alleging ineffective assistance of counsel in that her trial defense team failed to introduce evidence supporting Pike's alleged bipolar disorder. During this hearing, Shipp admitted to misinforming investigators and that he, in fact, was primarily responsible for Slemmer's murder. He stated that he was drunk and tired and just wanted the police to leave him alone when he put the onus of blame on Pike. Additional testimony from prior Job Corps student and the defendants' mutual friend Tyrone Comfort stated that Shipp controlled and abused Pike despite her assertions that he was the first male to protect her and she admired the respect and fear he elicited from others. Pike, however, was heavily medicated during this hearing for her alleged bipolar condition and the hearing was rescheduled for April 2008.

During her 2008 hearing, prosecutors portrayed Pike as a cold-blooded vicious killer who not only planned Slemmer's murder but prolonged it for sport, essentially playing cat-and-mouse with Slemmer by allowing her to get up and try to escape and then pushing her back on the ground for additional torture. Ultimately, her request for a new trial was denied.

Pike became newsworthy again in 2012 when she formulated an escape plan with the help of 34-year-old New Jersey resident Donald Kohut who frequently visited Pike in prison but the extent of their relationship remains unknown, and 23-year-old former prison guard Justin Heflin. In a joint investigation by the Tennessee Department of Corrections, the Tennessee Bureau of Investigation, and the New Jersey State Police after receiving information about the plan, both men were arrested and charged with bribery and conspiracy to commit escape, with Heflin charged with an additional facilitation to commit escape charge due to his job as a prison guard. Authorities discovered contraband evidence in the facility which could have only been brought in by a staff member and that Heflin was likely involved. Further investigation demonstrated that Heflin knew Kohut and that Heflin was receiving gifts and money for his assistance in the escape plan. Pike was also charged.

Even more recently, during yet another post-conviction relief hearing in 2015, testimony revealed that Pike was allegedly pregnant at the time of the murder. While this may be true it neither excuses her actions nor provides any potential evidence of legal insanity to justify an affirmative defense of not guilty by reason of mental disease or defect or guilty but mentally ill. Also during this hearing, Slemmer's mother requested the missing piece of her daughter's skull so she could bury the whole of her daughter but was denied as the skull piece remains a critical piece of evidence in Pike's ongoing legal appeals.

Since exhausting the state appeal process, Pike's new defense attorney, Assistant Federal Defender Stephen A. Ferrell, filed a

123-page petition on her behalf alleging that he constitutional rights were violated in both the original 1996 trial and penalty phase and that Tennessee's appellate courts ignored said violations. Among these claims is that capital punishment would amount to cruel and unusual punishment in violation of the Eighth Amendment of the United States Constitution because of Pike's youth, immaturity and mental illness. While Shipp—only 17 at the time of the murder—was too young to warrant imposition of a death sentence, Pike was not. Ferrell alleged that her trial lawyers were incompetent and failed to introduce evidence of mental illness, brain injury, and post-traumatic stress disorder. In response, the state Attorney General submitted a 90-page rebuttal repeatedly asserting that the state courts' ruling were all legally correct. As of the beginning of 2016, this battle continues.

Numerous video interviews of Pike over the past several years show her admitting that she was fully cognizant of her actions and that they were wrong. She stated that she felt as though she was taking out years of abuse on Slemmer and that she committed a horrible atrocity and deserves to be punished; however, she asserts that she deserves life without the possibility of parole for her actions; not the death penalty for the actions of three individuals. She has repeatedly stated that she wishes it was she who died and not Slemmer but such protestations are moot after the fact. One cannot help but wonder if Pike actually means what she says or is simply saying what she thinks others want to her. Knoxville Police Department detective Randy York who worked the case has said that in his lengthy career he has not encountered many people who he believes are evil but that Pike is, indeed, the personification of evil and that she should never be permitted to be around other human beings ever again.

Experts assert that the death penalty is not an effective general deterrent and debate over the morality and legality of capital punishment remains contentious and in the forefront of public discourse and debate. Currently, Tennessee is only one of 38 states which have the death penalty. Whereas women comprise 13% of those arrested for murder, only 2% are sentenced to death and, of those, only 3% are actually executed; primarily due to judges not wanting to sentence women to death. In Tennessee, only two individuals on death row have been executed—both males. The last time a woman was executed in the state was in 1837. Many currently believe that Pike will likely never be executed.

KILLER BABYSITTER : THE TRUE STORY OF CHRISTINE FALLING

33

DIANE ULLMER

It is said that cats have nine lives, most understand this as a mildly clever metaphor for the preternatural ability of felines to land on their feet.

The mentally challenged Christine Falling took this saying quite literally, so much so that during her formative years she would regularly take cats up to the top of the highest buildings in her Perry, Florida neighborhood and dropped them off over the roof.

Sometimes she would strangle them instead.

Most of the people that came in contact with her would walk away shaking their head in disbelief at her ignorance.

Stupidity would prove to be dangerous, however, as Christine would seek employment as a babysitter.

Tragically, she would soon graduate from killing cats to killing children.

Christine Laverne Slaughter was born on the 12th of March in 1963 to a poor and dysfunctional working class family in Florida. From an early age it was clear that she had a great deal of cards stacked against her, which included a large appetite, frontal lobe epilepsy (for which she had to take regular and powerful medication to prevent an epileptic attack or seizure) and an astonishingly low IQ.

Still, no one would notice the little girl walking down the street cradling different cats.

"She killed the cats," forensic psychologist Paula Orange said. "Because she wanted to take her rage out on something. Anything. Any small animal would do. She wanted to have power over life and death over something as she didn't have any power in her own life."

Both of her parents were poor and they would fight often. Some were petty outbursts while others turned violent. When these altercations turned physical, and they often did, the police would be called, time after time, typically with little repercussions.

Her father would also sexually abuse her in addition to administering daily beatings when she didn't please him.

"The loss of innocence came early for Christine," Orange said. "Her father was a sick pervert, pulling her into the bedroom as she was watching cartoons."

One day, after one of the daughter and father's incestuous meetings, Christine's father became suddenly irate and began to beat her with a bottle. Her mother rushed her to the hospital where she told an investigating officer that Christine had been in a car accident.

"A car done run her over," Christine's mother said. "I didn't get the license plate."

The physician that examined the little girl felt otherwise. The injuries were clearly caused by blunt force trauma but the police did not follow up.

"Christine and her sister were under the radar of child protective services," Orange said. "And they remained that way for a long, long time. The child protective service was not set up the way now. Christine was savaged as a young child. Like so many victims of sexual abuse, her wiring would change and she would be destined to some kind of tragic life, taking people along for the ride."

According to Christine sister, Carol, their parents were so aloof and detached from the rearing of their children that on one trip to the local supermarket, their mother, Ann Slaughter, simply decided to abandon them there. Shortly thereafter both girls were adopted by Dolly and Jesse Falling (thus adopting the last name over Slaughter). Dolly Falling always dreamed of having children but, due to physiological complications was completely incapable of doing so – for her, the sight of the Slaughter children was a godsend. Jesse Falling knew the Slaughters well and also readily accepted them into his home. However, this newest sanctuary was anything but, for not only did Christine's mental issues cause a lot of problems but there were also rumors that Jesse Falling would regularly sexually abuse the children.

These allegations were investigated and Jesse was twice arrested for allegedly sexually assaulting Carol. The allegations were never proven, however, and he served no jail time.

At the age of nine, both Christine and her sister Carol were taken from the Fallings. They were taken to a child care center located in Orlando following the intervention of a local pastor who worried about the two girls.

The Fallings hesitated with the request but eventually gave in to the advice of the pastor. Their new was called The Great Oaks Village of Orlando, a home for neglected and downtrodden children. Christine liked her new home despite making everyone around her feel awkward. She would often give her fellow children "strange looks" and walk the halls with a vacant gaze.

Christine also developed a habit of bursting out into sudden fits of rage that seemed wholly unprovoked, distressing the other children and caretakers. She was also extremely antisocial and would often move off to sit by herself, hardly ever conversing with any of the other residents of her new home.

"Her rage came about whenever she couldn't deal with something," Orange said. "Like a child crying over a broken toy or spilled milk. The problem was Christine was older now and still exhibiting child-like behavior."

At the age of only fourteen, Christine would marry a twenty-three-year-old man at the behest of her parents. The union was anything but a happy one, often devolving into heated shouting matches and violence.

Christine did not hold back during their physical altercations and on one occasion hurled a thirty-pound stereo at her beau's head.

They would separate only six weeks of wedded "bliss."

After the break-up, Christine would psychologically deteriorate even further. During this period of manic distress, Christine visited the hospital over fifty times yet the physician would never find anything wrong with her.

Nothing except hypochondria.

And yet, time after time, Christine continued to return to the hospital, every time with new and increasingly bizarre and outlandish symptoms.

ADULTHOOD

Christine grew into an oversized Baby Huey looking character as she grew old. She had a bulbous forehead and a child-like way of talking. Uneducated, she applied for jobs in restaurants and schools but was rejected. She held some menial jobs but could not last long in conventional employment.

Her epilepsy, child-like mannerisms and below average intelligence disqualified her from just about every line of work. Luckily, she was well liked by her neighbors, who saw in her an affable childish innocence, and she quickly found herself regularly assuming the role of babysitter for the community.

She had seemingly finally found her niche, gaining a reputation among the community as a caring and reliable babysitter.

"Her smile was disarming," Orange said. "Her demeanor was disarming. No one would suspect her of anything. In fact, she looked like someone who needed babysitting herself."

But on February 25th, 1980, everything changed.

Christine was asked to look after a playful child named Cassidy Johnson, a neighbor's kid.

Cassidy's parents left their child in the care of Christine without any trepidation. The child seemed to like Christine and they looked like they could get along.

A few hours later, however, Cassidy fell ill and was rushed to the doctor.

The initial diagnosis was that the child was suffering from encephalitis, the severe inflammation of the brain which is typically a condition brought on by very serious cerebral infections. The child languished in feverish oblivion for three terrifying days before dying.

The coroner's examination would reveal something else, however. The cause of the brain swelling was blunt force trauma to the girl's skull.

Only one person could have been responsible.

Christine Falling.

INTERROGATION

Christine tried to lie her way through the police questioning. She told them that the child had fallen from the crib and hit her head on the floor.

The police were not in the slightest convinced by there was no evidence to be had and no one else to corroborate or contest Falling's tale. The doctor who had attended to the child was suspicious himself and wrote a letter describing his misgivings to the cops.

His letter was lost and the case soon became forgotten...

MOVING TIME

Christine was smart enough to realize that she should not stick around. She moved to Lakeland, Florida which was becoming a bustling business center.

Christine settled in, finding a place to live in a trailer park where she would spend her days watching television and milling around outside her trailer, smoking and greeting passersby.

She returned to do the only work she knew; babysitting.

Finding work with the unsuspecting Davis family, she began watching over their four-year-old son Jeffery.

"Christine did have a playful side," Orange said. "She entered the Davis home and immediately to a shine to the young Jeffery. She pretended like she was a monster and began tickling the young boy. Jeffery's parents had no reason to suspect that she would do harm to him. Christine was a little slow but was young and could project a sweet persona when she needed."

Hours later, however, Jeffery's mother would come home to see Christine standing over her young son with a glass of Kool-Aid.

Her son was not breathing.

"What happened?" Jeffery's mother screamed.

"He stopped breathing."

"Don't just stand there," she screamed again. "Call an ambulance!"

Jeffery would be pronounced dead on arrival at the hospital.

An autopsy was performed but the cause of death was found to be a pre-existing heart condition which caused the life-sustaining organ to expand to an extremely unhealthy size. Upon further inspection, however, the coroner determined that the heart inflammation was not enough to cause this kind of sudden death. Failing to discover any other notable injuries or oddities of the child's physiology, the case was chalked up as a mysterious death.

Three days later, however, Christine would by hired to look after a young boy named Joseph Spring. His parents would be going to the funeral of the young Jeffery.

They had no idea that Christine was responsible for Jeffery's death.

Christine followed the same modus operandi as she did with young Jeffery. She was immediately able to charm the child with her own child-like qualities. She saw that the boy was interested in trucks and started to play "demolition derby" with him. His parents were satisfied that the child would be safe in her care and went to the funeral of Jeffery, their nephew who had been killed by their babysitter.

Joseph's parents left and after a few hours, the boy fell. He began crying and screaming which set off Christine.

"She couldn't handle frustration of any kind," Orange said. "She would pace back and forth, telling the boy to 'shush' but of course he doesn't listen. She can't handle it."

Christine experienced auditory hallucinations when her frustrations reached a peak. The voices in her head would tell her to 'kill' and 'make the child quiet.' She could not differentiate between the real voices and the voices in her head.

So she grabbed the nearest blanket and began suffocating the young boy.

"She was schizophrenic," Orange said. "You combine that with her low IQ and it is the recipe for disaster if she is watching a young child. She cannot parse out her rational thoughts from the voices in her head. This would lead to tragic consequences."

Like before, the coroner was puzzled by the death of a young and healthy boy. He speculated that

the cause of death might very well have been some undocumented, possibly new kind of viral infection. This theory would also account for the death of Jeffery Davis as well as Joseph since neither of them bore any marks of violence. Once again the coroner closed the case, dismissing it as a complete mystery.

"No one suspected Christine of anything," Orange said. "Her dumb and sweet persona actually worked in her favor. Nobody could suspect any malice to come out of her. She would smile and come across like an overgrown child. She didn't fit the mold of a child killer. On the surface, she had no sinister aspect about her."

Christine's reign of terror continued to go on unchecked as she moved to the town of Perry. This go around, however, she would become a caretaker rather than a babysitter. An elderly man named Wilbur Swindle needed someone to look after him and find a willing candidate in the smiling Christine.

On her first day of employment, however, the old man would be found dead.

Once again, the coroner would drop the ball, dismissing the old man's death due to a heart attack brought on by the failing health of old age.

There was no police inquiry.

"The killing of Wilbur Swindle seemed to be an anomaly in Christine's pattern of murder," Orange said. "For whatever reason, she had targeted young children. So the killing of Swindle looked to be a murder of opportunity. He probably did or said something to upset her. He was old and feeble and could easily be smothered down by the obese Christine."

TIME AWAY

Some time passed and Christine was contacted by her step-sister Geneva Daniels. Geneva had an eight-month-old daughter. They had not seen each other in awhile and Geneva invited Christine to go on a shopping trip.

On the way home, Geneva remembered that she needed some diapers. She parked outside the local store and ran in for only a minute.

She made the mistake of leaving the crying baby with Christine.

Moments later, an ear-piercing scream could be heard from the car. The louder the child screamed, the more agitated Christine became.

"Once again, her low frustration threshold kicked in," Orange said. "She simply never learned how to handle a stressful situation. What would seem like a mundane situation to a normal person, a baby crying, would seem like a life or death scenario to Christine. The more the baby cried, the less control she felt. Then she had to lash out."

She placed the baby's fuzzy blanket over its mouth and held it there until she stopped crying.

Her step-sister returned to the car only to find her eight-month-old baby girl in a lifeless heap in the arms of Christine.

Christine herself was crying, flailing her arms and hyperventilating.

"She stopped breathing," Christine said.

Her step-sister didn't suspect Christine at all.

Neither did the police.

"That is one of the reasons why Christine was able to commit these murders," Orange said. "She mastered the art of smothering, particularly with a loose material. It doesn't leave behind any marks or clues. It simply blocks the airways and the coroners are left grasping at straws."

JUSTICE AT LAST...

Christine's long, lengthy string of supernatural luck in avoiding suspicion came to a bitter and crushing end in the year of 1982.

Christine would meet a family who employed her to watch their ten-week-old son named Travis Coleman.

Travis would die under her care but initially, they held no suspicions toward Christine.

The coroner's exam would reveal that the child's death had not been some viral infection or cerebral swelling, but rather a strangulation!

Christine would go immediately to the hospital and check herself in. Her hypochondriac tendencies kicking in, she demanded that doctors find out what was wrong with her. She insisted that she was passing along a virus that was killing the children.

The physicians would find nothing wrong with her physically.

Finally, Christine told the doctor to call the police.

"I have something I want to tell them," she said.

Christine did not lie this time when faced with police questioning. She said she had killed her child using a method she described as "smotheration."

She then confessed to killing the other children using similar methods.

"Christine probably wanted to be caught at this point," Orange said. "She would confess while she was at the hospital. She wanted the burden off her back. Whatever it was inside her that was forcing her to kill those children, she wanted herself to be committed. In one moment of lucidity she probably realized what a danger she was to everyone around her."

When the police pressed the young woman as to why she had done such a heinous series of deeds she responded flatly that she had heard voices in her head.

These voices told her to use "soft, thick pillows and blankets" which were the reasons why there were no discernible and incriminating marks on her victims.

Christine spoke openly of hearing strange and seductive voices telling her to "kill the baby, kill the baby, kill the baby, kill the baby!"

These words would be repeated in her head, over and over like some kind of demonic mantra.

"I don't know why I done what I done," Christine said. "The way I done it, I seen it done on TV shows. I had my own way, though. Simple and easy. No one would hear them scream."

CONVICTION

Christine was able to avoid the death penalty but was instead sentence to a life term of imprisonment with the prospect for possible parole via joint committee decision in 2007. However, in 2006 the committee came to an early decision.

She had been behaving badly in prison, engaging in unpredictable and violent outbursts. The court then dismissed her chance for parole in its entirety.

The committee judged Christine to be a threat to the public (specifically children for obvious reasons) and declared that the safest and most forward thinking course of action is to keep her imprisoned to fulfill the rest of her term.

Christine Falling remains in dark and clanking confines of the well known Homestead Prison Complex of Miami and Dade County in the state of Florida.

Her story is perhaps a penultimate warning about the dangers of undiagnosed mental health issues and childhood abuse. If the history of such heinous crime in America tells us, it's that the combination of mental frailty and a past of physical and emotional ill-treatment is a cocktail that is not just dangerous, but deadly.

ALEXANDRA TOBIAS

45

DIANE THORSTON

On January 19th, 2010, 22 year old Alexandra Tobias was playing Farmville on Facebook at home in Jacksonville, Florida when she was interrupted by the cries of her three month old baby, Dylan. She tried to silence him by shaking him roughly – hitting his head in the process.

The child fell unconscious and she placed a frantic call to 911. The child would be taken to the hospital where he would die the next day. Alexandra would be arrested for second degree murder.

Just over a year later, on February 1st 2011, Tobias was sentenced to 50 years in prison.

"He who is the most defenceless among us was murdered by his own mommy. And why? Because he was crying during a game of Fishville or Farmville or whatever was going on during Facebooking time that day," the presiding Judge Adrian G Soud said.

In the time between the crime and the sentencing , news organizations across America picked up the story.

Why would Alexandra kill her baby?

EARLY LIFE

Tobias was born on August 11th 1988. Petite and thin, she was described by family and friends as 'fun-loving' and 'mischievous'.

Her parents divorced when she was five and one of her earliest memories was that of her mother throwing a plate at her father's head.'

Furthermore, Alex would reveal that she had been raped at a young age and her mother was often negligent in her care.

"My mom was severely bi-polar. When she was at her low, which was pretty often, she would try to kill herself. And she did try to commit suicide a couple of times and was admitted to a psychiatric hospital for the fact that her lows got so low," Tobias recalled.

"Alexandra felt rejection by her own mother," forensic psychologist Paula Martin said. "She thought that if her moher wanted to kill herself, if she wanted out of this life, then Alexandra herself must not be worth the trouble."

After a suicidal episode, Alexandra had confronted her mother with the admonition 'if you love me so much, then live for me.'

But on St Patrick's Day when she was 16, Tobias walked into her home to find her mom dead, having succumbed to heart disease. Her mother was dead on the couch and rigor mortis had set in. The television was on from the night before.

"It shattered me," Tobias recalled. "It broke me. I've never coped with it."

Domestic Troubles

Two years after her mother passed away and after she had graduated from Wolfson High School, Tobias met and began a relationship with EJ Edmondson. EJ was described by Alexandra as a "bad boy" and that she simply "fell for him because he didn't want a girlfriend."

The two would eventually move in together and she would become pregnant with Dylan. Alex put off her plans for college when she became pregnant with her son.

"I was thrilled," Tobias said after finding out she was pregnant. "I was scared more than anything."

But Tobias and Edmondson's relationship was far from stable. In fact, just three weeks before Dylan was killed, Tobias and Edmondson were arrested for a domestic conflict. Since Dylan was home, the Department of Children and Families (DCF) was supposed to have been informed of the incident. When questioned later, the DCF stated they had received an incomplete report. After the arrest, Tobias was given six months' probation and was told to attend an anger management class.

"Not only was her relationship unstable," Martin said. "But her mental status was unstable as well. Alex seemed to have suffered from post-partum depression as she began having suicidal ideations. She took it was a personal failure whenever the baby was sick or crying. When her boyfriend would come home, the baby would cry. So she began to connect his presence with the baby being unhappy."

"I wanted to kill myself," Tobias said. "I was tired of arguing with his father. I was tired of hurting on the inside. He was a newborn. Even though I wouldn't be there, I would no longer be a part of the equation that was hurting him."

Despite her rocky relationship with Edmondson, friends recall that Tobias was fiercely maternal towards Dylan. Jason Smith, a family friend told news organizations that Tobias would always take Dylan to a doctor if he had a cold or other minor illnesses.

"That girl was so protective over that baby. There should be more investigation done. I just don't know if she just snapped or what," Smith told the *Times-Union* in a phone call after the crime.

Tobias insisted that she loved motherhood.

"It was beautiful," Tobias said. "I couldn't get enough of him. I didn't want people touching him, I didn't want them to break him, I didn't want nobody to do anything to him. His cries were like music. They weren't really sad to me because that's him, that's his way of communicating. "

The Crime

On February 19th, however, Dylan's cries provoked a stronger, more ominous reaction from Tobias.

The day before the crime Tobias took a Facebook personality quiz which told her that she had a bipolar personality.

"Way to go, you crazy person," the quiz reported back. "You are too much for any one person to handle, including yourself."

"Alexandra certainly inherited her mother's manic episodes," Martin said. "She would become agitated, irrational, irritable then suddenly go to being depressed and even suicidal."

She was never formally diagnosed with bipolar disorder, however.

As her friends stated, her actions on February 19th contradicted her typical behaviour towards Dylan. On the day of the crime, she had taken Xanax, an anti-anxiety drug. She then logged on to Facebook and began playing Farmville, a simulation game create by Zynga where players assume the role of farmers ploughing land, growing and harvesting crops and caring for livestock. Players are invited to interact with their Facebook friends to earn rewards and virtual money - Farm Cash - to enhance the game experience.

Farmville was launched in 2009 on Facebook and was the social media's site most popular game in 2010 with millions of users across the world. Along with her affinity for Farmville, presentations in court, as well as media reports indicate that Tobias had a typical young adult's Facebook presence. She liked the Facebook pages for 'One Tree Hill' and 'Megan Fox', identified herself as a Christian and as a Republican.

She also had a profile for Dylan recording milestones; on January 1st she shared that he weighed 22 pounds and was 22 inches tall. She had joined a Facebook group opposing baby-shaking just a month before the crime.

Her online stand against baby-shaking was a direct contradiction to her actions on the day of the crime. While she was playing Farmville, Dylan began crying. After a while, infuriated by the continuous crying, Tobias shook Dylan roughly. She later told investigators she then paused to smoke a cigarette and believed that the family dog knocked Dylan off the sofa, causing him to start crying again. She picked him up and shook him again. A few minutes later she noticed he had stopped breathing and frantically called Dylan's father, followed by a call to 911. She followed the dispatcher's instructions and tried mouth-to-mouth resuscitation and chest compressions.

Despite hers and later the paramedic's efforts the next morning, 14 –week- old Dylan died, with head injuries - bruising on the skull and bleeding in the brain - and a broken leg. On the same day his mother was charged with aggravated murder.

Contradicting Stories

While Tobias first told the investigators that Dylan had been knocked off the sofa by the dog and hit his head, she later confessed that she had lost her temper at being interrupted by his cries while playing Farmville and shook him, hitting his head on the computer, while doing so.

"I got off the computer," Tobias recalled. "Took my pit bull outside, let him go to the bathroom and when - like - the next thing was more clear was the fact that he wasn't breathing in my arms anymore."

"I honestly can't recall the actual incident itself. But, when it comes down to it, I had taken a good handful of some Xanax...I guess I came to and realized that something wasn't right; I didn't know what it was in my arms...I realised that something I was holding before that was moving was no longer moving."

"Alexandra had to detach herself from the situation," Martin said. "She refers to her baby as 'something'. She can't bring herself to say 'my son' or 'Dylan.'"

Tobias also insisted doesn't remember shaking Dylan or hitting his head.

"She blamed the incident on her taking too much of the Xanax," Martin said. "Xanax can make you black out. But she 'came to' when she found out the baby wasn't breathing. So clearly the jury wouldn't give her a pass on that. She sipmly should not have been left in the care of an infant by herself. She was mentally unstable with a family history of bipolar disorder. Is it a failure of the system? It is a failure of Alex to not realize the warning signs in her own life and get professional help."

The Court Case

On October 29th, ten months after she was arrested, Tobias pleaded guilty to second degree murder.

This was following presentation of evidence, where prosecutors including Assistant State Attorney Rich Mantei used Facebook screenshots of Tobias' membership in the group against baby- shaking as well as other activities on Facebook as evidence. While Tobias told a psychologist she had blacked out during the incident, the prosecutors presented a recorded phone call from inside the prison where Tobias admits this was a lie.

"She was a young mother," Alexandra's sister Elizabeth said when she took the stand. "She was under a lot of stress, but I don't see her doing anything malicious. She knows better."

Tobias' grandmother, Irene Lane also testified, showing the courtroom a high school photograph of a fresh-faced Tobias.

Additionally, Stephen Bloomfield, a psychologist also testified, saying that Tobias had taken Xanax without a prescription, adding that it can heighten downward mood swings. He also commented on how her experiences with her bipolar mother could have caused an unhealthy frame of mind which was unable to cope normally with stressors.

Jan Abel, the defence lawyer asked the presiding judge Adrian G Soud to listen to the recording of the 911 call before making his judgement; the call featured a hysterical Tobias telling the operator her baby was not breathing.

Tobias herself told the judge that she had been suffering from postpartum depression, a condition where new parents suffer from mild clinical depression.

"I hate myself for what I did, but not for who I am," she said, going on to plead guilty to second degree murder. Tobias confessing was a part of a plea bargain where she would - on the judge's discretion - receive 25 to 50 years in jail. Her guilty plea saved the case from having to go through a jury trial which would have been extremely difficult for Tobias, Dylan's father as well as Earl Edmondson and Debra Edmondson, his grandfather and grandmother.

The Judgment

On February 1st, 2011, almost a year after Dylan died, Judge Soud sentenced Tobias to 50 years of prison, delivering his verdict alongside a chastizing reprimand.

Tobias in Jail

In her initial days in jail, reports from prosecutors in the case as well as the media highlighted how Tobias appeared to be trying to deny her role in Dylan's death.

A letter she sent to a male inmate was seen as evidence of this.

"I had a son named Dylan Lee, but he passed away on January 20, 2010! They are trying to charge me with my son's death and child abuse. Now I don't expect you to understand, but I can't really talk about it but I can tell you I'm in here for the wrong reasons."

Another inmate told prosecutor Mantei that Tobias spent time coloring, saying it was like she was in a home for girls.

"Alexandra really disassociated herself from the situation," Martin said. "She simply could not deal with what she had done so her initially her mindset was one of denial. Her behavior was not of a shell-shocked mother guilty for what she had done. She would blame everyone else, from the computer to the boyfriend to her grandmother and even the dog."

However, by 2015 when Candice DeLong interviewed her at the Lowell Correctional Institution in Ocala, Tobias' attitude had severely deteriorated; she seemed to have finally accepted her role in the crime and her responsibility for the crime.

"...I didn't come to terms with that it was actually me up until a couple of years ago. I had that realisation when I met my niece. She opened my eyes to the life that I took and the choice that I took to have drugs...When I see my sister with my niece. It breaks my heart. It still breaks my heart. She's so good with her and I know I'd be like that with my son. It's something I have to live with for the rest of my life...I don't need to run from it anymore. I need to face it."

Tobias goes on to confide that she deals with what she has done by self-mutilation, saying that this allows her to focus on the physical pain rather than the more crippling emotional pain. "I hurt somebody. So, the way I hurt somebody is the way I hurt myself," Tobias revealed.

"It helps (self-mutilation). But its something I have to constantly go through. Its not just something that I, have to go through one day. I don't want to feel those feelings so instead of embracing them I'll inflict them."

Alexandra plans on self-mutilating herself for along time. She has not forgiven herself and doesn't think she ever will.

The Media's Judgment

Some of the news report during the court case as well as after Judge Soud delivered his judgement mirrored 'Tobias' inability to forgive herself. While 'Tobias' interview indicates self-condemnation, many reports also scathingly condemned her.

Gawker wrote a brief paragraph on her crime, ending the summary with the word 'yeesh'. Meanwhile, HollywoodLife, another popular website reported the crime and commented "Disgusting. I can't stomach this kind of abuse. Considering that so many of my friends and family are struggling to conceive, it really enrages me that mothers can be so careless with the kids they were blessed to have."

What perhaps drew the most attention to the case was the fact that it was discussed for nearly an hour on the CNN show '*Nancy Grace On CNN Headline News*'.

Transcripts from the show concerning Tobias include several call-ins from experts in fields relating to the case - these include prosecutor Richard Mantei and Dr Leigh Vinocur of the University of Maryland School of Medicine. The transcripts also indicate that the show re-created the 911 call Tobias placed after she realized that Dylan had stopped breathing.

"Bombshell tonight," Nancy Grace said in opening her segment on Tobias. She would go on to sensationalize the story, stating that Tobas was a 'Mommy addicted to Facebook's Farmville' and spent hours 'living in her imaginary world with imaginary friends on an imgainary farm.' She then 'bludgeoned the little baby in the head, with what else, her computer.'

The show also pointed to evidence that Tobias had developed a romantic interest in prison where she wrote letters to a male inmate asking him all about himself - his favourite color, his favorite car, what kind of music he's into and his age. Nancy Grace read out part of one letter on air: "Hey, baby. I hope you had a good weekend. Thanks for the compliment and the beautiful Valentine's picture. To tell you the truth, I've had my eye on you since I've been here, but too shy to do anything about it. I think you're sexy as hell."

Additionally, the show brought out other aspects of Tobias' behaviour following the crime. According to Mantei, she called a neighbor from the hospital Dylan was being treated at, asking him to go into their house and hide her marijuana stash and pipe.

Grace and other commentators spent a considerable amount of time discussing Farmville, as well as Fishville, which Tobias also played. One commentator highlighted how checking in to both one's farm and one's aquarium (in Fishville) regularly was important to tend to the crops, fish and livestock. He went on to suggest that Tobias, having already invested a large amount of time in tending to her crops and her fish, would have been extremely frustrated at the interruption.

In '*Cyber Effect: A Pioneering CyberPscycholgist Explains How Human Behaviour Changes Online*' by Dr Mary Aiken, a forensic cyber-psychologist, Aiken briefly mentioned Tobias' case, using it to begin exploring the role of technology in the escalation of an explosive act of violence. "Can we say that Alexandra Tobias was addicted? Is the explanation that simple? Her virtual cattle were doing fine, but her real life was in ruins." Aiken commented.

Similarly, several other media organizations focused on the role that an online gaming addiction had to play in Tobias' crime.

However, EJ, the baby's father was displeased about this approach. "That is insulting," Edmonson said. "It wasn't about Facebook. It was about my son."

"The media focused almost exclusively on the social media aspect of the case,"Martin said. "The fact that she was on Facebook and on Farmville made for good copy because it was so popular. This was more of a case of a violent bipolar personality who was alone with a baby."

The Aftermath

Indeed, Tobias' case was not just a case of an internet game addiction that went horribly wrong. It was a combination of factors including online influence and mental instability which resulted in Tobias snapping and Dylan losing his life.

"If you feel like you're unstable; mentally, physically - whatever it might be, don't ignore it," Tobias said, trying to warn other young women. "Don't ignore it, don't think that you can make it better because sometimes you need a little extra...to help you, to seek that help because if I would have seeked the proper help, my state of mind might not have been where it was at and my son would have never been put in that predicament."

Tobias is currently in prison, and as of this writing is almost six years into her 50 year sentence.

CHILD KILLER MAGGIE YOUNG

JAMES FALCON

Who was Maggie Young?

Maggie Young's case is relatively unknown today. In fact, even at the time, it did not seem to receive the attention that it perhaps deserved. This was undoubtedly, at least in part, due to the fact that Maggie and her young family lived in Hawaii. News travelled fast around the island, of course, but the mainland didn't pay all that much attention. The story was covered in newspapers across the country, but after the story was first told on page ten or worse, reporters showed little interest. Almost none of them covered the story of what happened after Maggie's arrest.

Moreover, this is a case which took place more than fifty years ago now, in 1965. Believe it or not, this was a time when serial killers, true crime and murder mysteries didn't receive as much attention as they do today. Take, for example, Casey Anthony: she has spawned a decade of public outrage which has seared itself onto America's cultural consciousness. But Maggie Young didn't, not way back in 1965. Hers was just another story.

Just like Casey Anthony- and if anything, exactly like Andrea Yates- Maggie Young killed her own children. She drowned them, one by one in the bathtub, and laid them back out on their beds afterwards... But unlike Yates, Young didn't live out the rest of her life between four padded cell walls. Maggie's life became unbearable after her medical treatment helped her to overcome her delusions, and she realised what she had done to her loving family. She escaped from the oversight of medical staff, took off across the grounds of the facility, and took her own life.

That was the end of the story for almost four decades, until the story of Andrea Yates hit headlines. James Young stepped into the spotlight to help people- and Russell Yates, Andrea's husband- understand what it is like to lose your family to the hands of a loved one, and live with the consequences. Since interrupting his private life to help others overcome post-partum depression and post-partum psychosis, he went quickly back and disappeared from the radar once more. And, since, that has truly been the end of the story.

Maggie's descent into mental illness

The case occurred so long ago now, in a time before the advent of the internet or even cell phones, that finding any published information on Young is actually a difficult task. Before she took her children's lives with her own hands, little to nothing is known about Maggie, her home life, or her former husband James Young. We do know that she was an ash blond, and that her family had moved to Hawaii a generation before. Maggie's mother, Mrs. Chauncey Brown, lived in North Augustus, South Carolina.

Maggie, her husband James and their five children lived on Nalopaka Place, in the suburb of Aiea in Honolulu. The area has a population comparable to a small town, of around 10,000 today but undoubtedly fewer then. The area is North West of the main city, and is actually quite close to Pearl Harbor. Part of the suburb, Aiea Heights, enjoys wonderful views of the bay; Nalopaka Drive is too close to the sea to have any real view at all. Aloha Stadium, home of the University of Hawaii Rainbow Warriors and the largest stadium on any of the islands, is a minute's walk away (although it wasn't opened until 1975).

The couple lived with their five youngest children. Maggie had two adult children, who she had raised in a previous marriage. Counting all of her children, Maggie had six daughters and one son. Her youngest was just eight months old in November 1965, and her eldest with James was an eight year old son. In 1965, their children were Jessica, an eight month old daughter; Jeanette, 2 years old; Judith, 3 years old; Janice, 5 years old, and James Frank Jr., who was 8. Maggie's husband James was an Air Force captain, stationed at Hickam Air Force Base near Honolulu.

What information we do have comes from James Young himself, and a select few news stories from the Honolulu Star-Bulletin. Maggie was born around 1927, which made her 38 years of age when she committed the crimes which gave her a notorious place in history. Prior to her crimes, just like Andrea Yates, Maggie was sent to hospital several times for her mental illness in the years leading up to the last major event of her life.

James Young described the situation in detail, many years later. He wrote that she had very slowly and gradually begun to exhibit signs of depression, which eventually became a completely psychotic state. According to James, she was tired all the time due to her awkward sleeping schedule, which took in all hours of the day; she would even sleep in her clothes.

"Her behavior slowly changed until nothing I nor the children did was right," he wrote. After months of deterioration, Maggie was unable to take care of her youngest children- her children with James. Of course, this being the early 1960's, the fact that Maggie was at least temporarily unable to care for her children was a bigger deal than it would be today. They were not taken into care, but left to Maggie's two eldest children, her two adult daughters. These two daughters did not live at home with their mother, but had long since left and gotten married. They would visit when they could, and juggled care between them.

"After they left, I would come home to find the children in dirty or wet diapers. I would change them, give them their baths and get them ready for bed. During all this she [Maggie] would be in bed," Young wrote. James was an Air Force captain, who flew regular missions and could be gone for days at a time. Perhaps because of his time spent away from home, James found it difficult to recognize that Maggie was suffering from a mental illness of some kind.

As her descent continued, and Maggie did not find the support she needed, she began to have hallucinations and visions. As Maggie and her family were very devout people, these visions were often religious in nature. One night, for instance, she left her family alone and disappeared for over three hours. When she finally came home, she claimed that she had come back from church- having been to marry Jesus Christ. When she talked with her husband about what had happened, she wasn't clear, but she told James that the Virgin Mary was now his grandmother.

Even accounting for her love for her religion, it was clear that Maggie was suffering with debilitating delusions. It was clear that she would be unable to continue playing any role in caring for her children. Not long after her disappearance, she attacked her husband with a broom as he tried to leave for work one morning. She shouted at him: according to James, "she said, 'They are out there. They have come to kill me.'"

Rather than leave his wife, James stayed home that day. He wanted to have his wife committed, for her safety and for his own, and for the safety of their family. Maggie was unpredictable, delusional and beginning to exhibit signs of violence. No matter what the diagnosis would prove to be, she was becoming more of a risk day by day.

But James was pushed back when he called the hospital. He was told that in order for his wife to be committed, she would have to go to the hospital and commit *herself* voluntarily. Quite naturally this seemed like an impossible task at first, but with the help of their priest and their family doctor, James managed to convince Maggie that it was for her own good. She agreed to go- as much as she could have agreed to anything in the state that she was in.

James described what happened next. "She was in the hospital at least a month to six weeks when the psychiatrist told me there was nothing more he could do for her. Any improvement would have to come at home," he wrote in an email to the Star-Bulletin many years later. Again, this was the middle of the 1960's: psychiatric care and medication was not as advanced as it is today, and even now it can be difficult to achieve positive outcomes with a large amount of patients that need mental health care.

"When Maggie was in the hospital, I prayed a lot. Mostly I prayed that she would come home to us. When she did come home, and in a few weeks drowned the children, I blamed the Almighty. Then I realized that my prayers were answered. I should have prayed for her recovery," he wrote. "Then I blamed myself." Maggie had not been ready to come home, but since the medical professionals of the state hospital felt that they could do nothing more for her, she had been sent away anyway; nobody knew precisely what terrible effects that this would have.

The Murders

The murders took place bright and early in the morning. Ed Young was away on another mission, and neither of Maggie's eldest daughters was visiting that day. At 8am, Maggie sent her eldest son to school, and wasted no time in systematically, almost robotically drowning her children. Like Andrea Yates, she drowned them one by one in the bathtub, starting with the eldest and finally killing her youngest last. Her youngest daughter wasn't yet a year old.

Afterwards, she walked to her son's school to bring him home. At 9:30am, he arrived, and Maggie drowned him too. At some point after that, Maggie arranged her children in their beds. When the police arrived later that day, Maggie told the officers that she had been distraught due to her inability to care for her children. She told case investigator John Dickson: "I killed my children". There was no doubt as to what had happened.

She was taken to Honolulu City County Jail, and awaited arraignment on a charge of first degree murder. Even though it was obvious she had killed each of her children in turn, she was only charged with murdering her son, James. Officers charged her within four hours, aware that she was still being treated as an outpatient by the Tripler Army Hospital she had been at from July to September.

A family friend, Mrs. Elaine Marshall of Honolulu, told police that Maggie had called her shortly after the murders. According to Mrs.

Marshall, Maggie asked her about the penalty for murder in Hawaii. Mrs. Marshall said "Oh no, Maggie, what have you done?" to which she replied "I killed them. I killed them all. They were crying. They were crying and I couldn't take care of them all. They were sick and they were crying."

After the call, Mrs. Marshall had immediately contacted the police. Detectives Robert Davidson and Joe Luna rushed to the scene and paid a visit to the family's house, where Davidson asked Maggie: "What seems to be your trouble?" But after a few moments it became obvious what the trouble was. Maggie told them "I killed my children. I drowned them," and the two officers quickly discovered the children, lying in two beds in one of their rooms.

Autopsies done on the bodies over the next few days confirmed that each of them had died by drowning, meaning that in combination with Maggie's many confessions there could be no doubt what had happened- only what punishment should be handed out. Mrs. Marshall told investigators that before she had received Maggie's call that day, she had already been worried that a tragedy might occur because of Maggie's inability to take care of her children.

Another neighbor described Mrs. Young as "very nice", and claimed that the children were good, and always well behaved. Maggie, she said, was always friendly but had appeared more nervous than usual after Jessica was born, the previous December. The family had shown few signs to the outside world that there was a pressure building up; a pressure that would crack and result in the deaths of their five innocent children.

Maggie is committed to the State Hospital

Maggie had spent two months at the Tripler Army Medical Center earlier that year, after her mental breakdown. She was initially held on a charge of first degree murder, but this charge was quickly dropped because of Maggie's obvious delusions. Considering her previous experience with mental illness, court psychiatrists and even the prosecution felt that it would be unfair to try her as if she were in her right mind.

She was charged only with drowning her son, despite having already admitted to killing all of her children. Because she met the criteria of having acted under 'a diseased and deranged condition', she was deemed unfit to stand trial. So rather than be forced to sit in the dock and defend actions she wouldn't even be able to describe, she was immediately sent to the State Hospital, which is still in Kaneohe to this day.

According to hospital administrators, Maggie began to respond to her treatment early on. At this point in time, the Hawaii State Hospital was undergoing radical changes. According to Joanne Lundstrom, a psychiatric social worker working there at the time, the era of 'snake-pit' institutional care for the mentally ill 'was gone, but not too far removed'. During her time there, Lundstrom took part in reorganising the hospital and improving the ways that it cared for patients.

One of the ways in which patient care began to improve was through the use of modern medicines that could help treat psychiatric disorders. Joanne Lundstrom said that they had 'a tremendous impact' when they were introduced, and they were instrumental in helping Maggie Young overcome her delusions and mental illness generally. Today, these kinds of medicines are used to great effect in the treatment of schizophrenia and delusions, just like Maggie had. The only alternative prior to this kind of medication were treatments like electro-shock therapy and frontal lobe lobotomies, which gave less than optimal results.

Unfortunately another hospital administrator, Audrey Mertz, described how Maggie had just begun responding positively to her medication and treatment when the enormity of what she had done began to sink in. It was too much for Maggie. Six months after she was first committed to the hospital, on July 25th 1966, she went AWOL while on a pass to walk around the grounds alone.

She was found soon after, having hung herself from the rafters of a chicken slaughtering shed on the hospital's grounds. It is difficult to imagine the pain she must have felt upon truly understanding what she had done, and finally realising that her children were gone. To lose five children would be a burden that would lead many to a similar end, let alone the burden of living with the guilt if you, as a parent, had ended your own children's lives. Dr. Audrey Mertz spoke to the press after Maggie's suicide, and told them that "the more she improved, the more her realization of her act. She was up against a dead end."

James did not want to speak with press at the time. Although the story was not covered extensively by press on the mainland, the Honolulu Star-Bulletin and other Hawaiian newspapers certainly thought that it would make interesting news for their readers. James Young was, and always has been, a private the delusions Maggie had for what had happened. He couldn't bring himself to blame his wife, even though he had lost his children.

'In her mind she had removed the children from a cruel world and had sent them to a far better place to be with God. I think that the proof that she truly believed this is demonstrated in the fact that as her treatment slowly returned her to reality, she began to realize that what she had done was terribly wrong and eventually she could no longer live with the terrible truth.'

James leaves Hawaii, and reaches out to the press

James Young left Hawaii shortly after the deaths of his children at the hands of his wife. He moved back to the mainland, to California, and allowed the case to be forgotten by history: by all accounts, he is an intensely private man who would rather leave that sad period of his life behind him. That, of course, is completely understandable. Since he left Hawaii, he remarried, although he did not have children again.

But when Andrea Yates killed her children in 2001, suddenly, the media began to draw parallels between the two cases. Of course, they shared many similarities- right down to the way that the poor children were killed. Specifically, Honolulu Star-Bulletin reporter Treena Shapiro wrote an article for the newspaper which brought the old case to light. In that report, she quoted an email interview which she conducted with James Young, who she had asked for quotes on how it must feel to lose your family to the hands of a loved one.

James, who had not sought out the media and had not been sought out in turn, was helpful. He was 72 years of age when Yates' story became national news, and perhaps enough time had passed that he seemed happier to talk with the press. He wrote that he hoped that in finally speaking out about the tragedy that had befallen his family, he could encourage others to get help for post-partum depression. He had reached out to the Star-Bulletin by email.

"Since I am the father of those Aiea children, I feel compelled to do what I can to help this woman who is a victim of postpartum depression and the terrible feeling of inadequacy she must have felt—the same feelings my late wife must have felt. Behavior signs we all recognized in hindsight," Young wrote in his first email. "Medical science needs to recognize this condition earlier and help the mother before it develops into paranoid schizophrenia, as it did in the case of Maggie."

"This ill woman does not need to be sentenced to prison; certainly not charged with first-degree murder," he continued. "My wife was charged with first-degree murder. But Hawaii justice recognized her illness and gave her the medical help she needed. Unfortunately she did not survive the cure." Considering that the cure had helped Maggie to realise what she had done, it would perhaps have been kinder to allow her to remain delusional and to never understand the gravity of the crime she had committed.

In a message to Yates' husband, James wrote "[a]ll I can say to him is there is no 'closure' but there is life after tragedy." Young told the newspaper that he managed to survive his ordeal through relying on the support of his family, friends and co-workers. "We need to recognize postpartum depression with psychosis earlier and successfully treat it," he wrote. "We must do whatever we can to prevent another mother killing her children."

Russell Yates reaches out to James

Even though the story only appeared in the Hawaiian press and on the Star-Bulletin's website, Andrea Yates' husband found it and reached out to the newspaper to try and get in touch with James. Although Russell Yates was not allowed to speak out about *anything* related to his wife's case because of a court order, he told Treena Shapiro that he had reached to James and the two had been able to connect over their shared sorrows. The two had spoken over the telephone. "He was encouraging to me and supportive of my wife and me," Yates told Shapiro.

In another email interview with the Star-Bulletin after the two had first spoken, Young wrote that "[a] tragedy resulting from this illness must not occur again. There must be better awareness of the seriousness of this illness." He was, of course, writing about post-partum depression. Young told Shapiro that he had tried to support Yates. Andrea Yates had been on suicide watch since the murders, and was at the time facing the prospect of the death penalty.

According to Shapiro, writing in the Star-Tribune, "Young said he told Yates to keep his faith, not to be ashamed to cry and to be prepared to cope with the pain for the rest of his life. There is no such thing as closure, he said." Considering that Young was 72 at the time that he wrote to Yates, there could be little else that would as accurately convey the horror of what happened that Young still felt no closure after all those years. "I still cry and had my share of tears following his tragedy," Young wrote to Shapiro. "After all these years the tears come less frequently but I have days and nights."

"Christmas is also very difficult. Memories come flowing back. Christmas is for the children. Without them, Christmas is not the same," he continued. Young and Yates shared memories of their kids, which Young told him to cherish. After remarrying, James chose not to have any more children, a decision which his new wife supported. "After I remarried, my wife was understanding and comforting," he wrote.

He also connected with Yates over the way that people take their families for granted, and that before you know it, they could be gone. "I told him that for years, I would experience anger every time I saw someone humiliating a child in public, especially in restaurants. I wanted to tell the abusing parent that they should enjoy their children," Young wrote. "Their time together may be shorter than they think."

James followed the Yates' case in the press, and was disappointed with the guilty verdict that she initially received. Young again wrote to Shapiro, and told her that he had been driving home from work at the time he had heard the news. "To say I was disappointed is a great understatement," he wrote. "I have been following the Houston Chronicle coverage of the trial on a daily basis, and based on the coverage I have read, I could not believe a jury would find her guilty. Even the prosecution's expert witness had left the door open for an insanity verdict."

He had previously written to Shapiro, and had then too talked about the horrible effects of post-partum depression and psychosis, and how important it was that the symptoms of these conditions were recognised and treated as soon as possible. 'I don't mean to say that all parents who kill their kids are innocent by reason of insanity. But those suffering from SERIOUS (postpartum depression) do not need to be in jail. They need to be given treatment,' he wrote. 'Hopefully, the treatment will come before the tragedy.'

Young was a Texas native before having moved to Hawaii for the Air Force, and his children are buried at the Fort Sam Houston National Cemetery. As such, it was no surprise that he felt so strongly about the Yates case. He wrote that he was ashamed of "the Wild West 'hang 'em high' mentality—especially in the Houston courts." "Under the circumstances, I am pleased. ... At least she will receive treatment. I can't help but feel sorry for her and Rusty," he wrote.

Since the Yates case, Young went back to the solitude of the life he had built after the terrible events that tore apart his first family. He was 72 going on 73 at the time, and since the Yates case was over fifteen years ago now, that would be another fifteen years added to his already long life. Although what happened to his young family is not well known, even despite the comparisons that were made between that and what happened to Russell Yates, it's certain that any reader who encounters his sad story could only wish him happiness in this life, or the next.

CHILD KILLER ANDREA YATES

JAIME FOSTER

Andrea Yates

Andrea Yates was, and still is, a devoutly religious woman. She did, and still does also suffer from severe depression and could justifiably be called 'insane'. In fact, that's what she's been called by the courts- for having murdered her young family, one by one, in one of the most shocking criminal cases in recent American history.

Her crime was drowning each of her five children over the course of just one hour, before laying them down in bed as if to sleep. She was initially found guilty of murder, but her charge was changed at her retrial to innocent by reason of insanity. She was then committed to North Texas State Hospital, a high-security facility, and finally to a low security state mental hospital where she remains to this day.

The reason why Andrea chose to kill her children stemmed from her insanity, but expressed itself through her religion. Andrea had always been devout, but had been inspired by her religion and her delusions that her children had been inhabited by demons. It was this that had led her to kill her children on that fateful day.

Andrea Yates' background

Andrea was born July 2nd, 1964, and lived in Houston, Texas during her childhood. She was the youngest sibling from a total of five, and born to Irish and German immigrants. Her friends say that she has suffered from depression since at least her late teenage years, although there were no signs of what would happen because of her mental illness later in life.

By all accounts, she was successful at school, and graduated as class valedictorian from Milby High School 35 years ago, in 1982. She quickly found a job through a two year long nursing program, and went on to work at a University of Texas cancer center for eight years, until 1994. It was during this time that Andrea met Rusty, her husband to be; they met when they were both 25 years old, and living in the same apartment block. Rusty would later recount how they met to the judge and jury, and say how he had no idea how the woman he had met that day could have become the woman in front of him then.

Andrea and Rusty were quickly married, and just as quickly decided to have as many children as God would allow. By 1999, the couple had just had their fourth child, Luke. Their others were named Noah, John, Paul and Luke. A year later, they would have their first girl- Mary. But far from enjoying their blessings, as most families would, Rusty began to notice that Andrea had become depressed.

From 1999 until the murders, which took place in 2001, Andrea showed signs of severe postpartum depression and dreadful delusions. One day in June 1999, Rusty came home to find that his wife had attempted suicide by an overdose of pills. He had come home just in time, and took her to the hospital, where she was prescribed a course of anti-depressants. But this was just the beginning of a downward spiral.

Not long afterwards, Andrea threatened suicide again- this time holding a knife to her own neck, and begging her husband to let her die. Rusty once more took her to the hospital, where she was prescribed the anti-psychotic medication Haldol. She did appear to be getting better for a while, and the family moved to their first house (they had previously been living in a small motor home).

But just a month after her first episode, Andrea suffered a complete breakdown. This time, she attempted suicide twice, whereupon she was finally diagnosed with postpartum psychosis by her psychiatrist, Dr. Eileen Starbranch. Starbranch appeared in court after the murders, and testified that she had encouraged the couple not to have any more children since it would effectively guarantee similar psychotic episodes in the future; but the pair did not want to listen, and conceived their final child (Mary) just seven weeks after Andrea was discharged from hospital.

Because of the birth of her new child, Andrea stopped taking her medication. But she nevertheless seemed stable- at least, until the death of her father in March, 2001. It was at this point that she began to truly circle the drain. She stopped feeding Mary, began to self-harm and spent the majority of each day reading the Bible and doing little else. It got to the point where she required hospitalization, but upon her release it seemed that nothing could rouse her from her psychotic state.

It was then that Andrea first began to seriously consider killing her own children. In May, she drew a bath- just like she would a month later- with the intent of killing them. She even confessed this to her husband Rusty, who of course took her back to her doctor, Dr. Mohammed Saeed; but Dr. Saeed concluded that she had drawn the bath to drown herself, and didn't take Rusty's concerns seriously. Of course, it was on June 20th of that year that she committed her terrible crime.

The killings

From the outside, the family seemed to have been blessed with their children, and seemed happy too. Neither Andrea nor Rusty let on to their friends and neighbors that they were having any difficulties at all. Their children were always neat and well dressed, Rusty worked a steady career job, Andrea was a capable homemaker and home-schooler. But this image was shattered on June 20th, 2001.

According to Andrea herself, in statements she gave to police, she drowned her children one by one in their family bathtub. She stated that she started with her younger sons first, since they were less likely to put up any fight; she then began to drown her daughter, just six months old, when her eldest walked in and asked- 'What's wrong with Mary?'

When her eldest, Noah, realised what his mother was doing, he ran. He tried to escape from the family home, but didn't get far, as Andrea chased and caught him. He was then drowned too, while Mary's body was still floating next to him in the bathtub. It is hard to imagine anything more horrific.

It was Andrea that called the police, saying that she needed an officer right away- although she wouldn't say why. When the police officers did arrive, she immediately confessed: 'I just killed my kids'. Noah was still in the bathtub, and the other three were arranged in their beds as if they were sleeping, Mary in the arms of one of her brothers.

Officers found the family dog tied up in the backyard. Rusty later said that when he had left that morning- which was a matter of minutes before Andrea drew a bath to drown her children- the dog had been outside, but not tied up. During the trial it was claimed that Andrea had consciously stopped the dog from being able to do anything about her plans. But whatever the case, she was taken into custody for what seemed like an open and shut charge- of having murdered her children.

Yates was held at Harris County Jail and was placed on suicide watch. At this point, prosecutors were unsure as to whether they wanted to pursue the death penalty or not, or whether they would be successful if they did; although that being said, Harris County is well known for its administration of the death penalty, since they have put a grand total of 62 people to death since 1977. For context, that would place it third compared to a list of entire *states*, behind only Texas (of which Harris County is a part) and Virginia.

While the prosecution were deliberating, the defense was already certain that they would plead not guilty, on the grounds of Andrea's psychosis. George Parnham, Yates' attorney for her defense, claimed that for a month after her arrest it was impossible to talk to Yates at all due to her inability to interact rationally with anybody, even her partner Rusty.

The Trial

Yates' case depended on a specific Texas law. In Texas, for a defendant to plead the defense of insanity, they have to be able to prove that they could not tell the difference between right and wrong (at least, at the point in time when the crime was committed). This is perhaps the most stringent check on the use of the insanity defense anywhere in the United States.

This law meant that even though Yates' lawyers could bring up her repeated suicide attempts and her repeated psychiatric hospitalization, these facts actually weren't enough for a successful defense on their own. No matter how ill, and no matter how delusional Yates may have been, if the prosecution could prove that Yates knew what she had been doing was wrong then the courts would have no choice but to sentence her as they would a person in their right mind.

Because of the importance of this element to the case, the prosecution decided to bring in perhaps the most famous psychiatrist practicing today, and no stranger to court cases like these, Dr. Park Dietz. Dietz should be well known to anybody who follows these sorts of cases: he gave testimony in the trials of the Unabomber, Susan Smith (who also killed her children through drowning) and John Hinckley, the would-be assassin of Ronald Reagan.

Most famously, Dietz worked on the case of Jeffrey Dahmer, when he successfully convinced the court to find him legally sane. If anybody could convince the jury to convict Andrea as a sane women, the prosecution thought, it would be Dietz. His testimony lasted two days, and was the media highlight of the trial. He gave a Powerpoint presentation to clarify the reasons why, he argued, Andrea should be found guilty as she was legally sane at the time.

During his testimony, the courts showed recorded footage of interviews that Dietz conducted with Andrea. "Before you did it, did you think it was wrong?" Dietz asked.

"No," Andrea replied.

"Why did you not think it wrong?"

Andrea answered, "If I didn't do it, they would be tormented by Satan."

It almost seems backwards: Andrea's legal sanity was proven by her delusions. But for the courts of Texas, this proved to be enough. In March, 2002, the jury had little choice but to find her guilty of murder due to the fact that she was legally sane at the time of the crimes according to Texas law, rightly or wrongly. The prosecution had been intent on seeking the death penalty, but the jury rejected the option. She was, instead, sentenced to life in prison with a chance of parole after 40 years. In effect, Andrea was guaranteed to be in prison for almost the entirety of her adult life.

Appeal and retrial

Even though the case for Andrea's guilt was unassailable, the defense nonetheless managed to order a retrial based on a charge of false testimony, levelled against Dr. Dietz. The defense claimed that Dr. Dietz had either lied or made a mistake during his testimony, with regards to an episode of Law & Order which he claimed could have inspired Andrea's actions. The only problem was that no such episode, which Dr. Dietz had claimed bore remarkable similarities to the story of Andrea's crimes, had been aired.

"Shocked at the possibility of having made a factual error, even one unrelated to Mrs. Yates, I immediately researched the issue, with help from the writers and producers of 'Law & Order,' and within hours determined that my recollection was probably incorrect," Dietz wrote in a statement explaining what had happened. An author, and one-time writer for *Law & Order* Suzanne O'Malley reported to the press that no such episode as Dietz had described had ever been aired.

O'Malley spoke to CBS News' *The Early Show* that Yates could now understand what she had done, but had nonetheless (in her opinion, based on letters she had received from her) been legally 'insane' at the time of the crimes. "She understands what happened. It's a living nightmare for her. I don't think she'll ever forgive herself. She asks her husband, Rusty Yates, how he forgives her. And he said, 'Andrea, if I were in a car driving the five children and I had a heart attack and had a wreck and they all died, would you blame me? Would it be my fault?' and she said, 'No.' He said, 'That's the same thing with you. You're mentally ill. It's a brain sickness.'"

In fairness to Dietz, he had written to the prosecution long before the retrial, in a letter dated March 2002. He admitted in the letter that he had made a mistake, possibly confusing two different episodes with one another, and thus given incorrect testimony during the trial. These two episodes were on Susan Smith and a young girl who had killed her baby after it was born instead of admitting that she had been pregnant. Both of these episodes were shown in the weeks leading up to Andrea's murder of her children. The letter that Dietz wrote to prosecutors was never brought to the attention of the trial. Once the information came out, however, the appellate court found that a retrial would be necessary because of the profound influence that Dietz had had on the outcome of the original trial.

The focus of the retrial was once again on Andrea's mental health and the actions of those around her that may have exacerbated her illness. At the trial, Rusty admitted to having left Andrea alone, despite it being recommended no to. He said that he and the rest of her family hoped that it would give her greater independence and confidence, and eventually help her to fulfil her role as a mother. But she still showed signs of mental difficulties throughout this time, for instance when she tried feeding Mary solid food, choking her, when she was still far too young.

Some of Andrea's family were supportive of the idea, but others, not so much. Her brother Brian Kennedy appeared on Larry King after the trial to recall that Rusty had told him he hoped that leaving her alone would give Andrea a 'swift kick in the pants', and motivate her to improve her own life. Andrea's psychiatrist, Dr. Starbranch, also expressed her dismay at the pair's plans to try to improve Andrea's mental health. In particular, during a visit just prior to her being discharged as a patient, the couple told Dr. Starbanch that they planned on having more children despite her opposition to the idea.

At the trial, Rusty claimed that he had not known the effects that these actions would have in the long run. 'If I'd known she was psychotic, we'd never have even considered having more kids,' he told the press during the trial. He also expressed his regret at not having seen the signs of her illness appearing sooner.

Without the influence of Dietz's testimony, Yates was this time found not guilty by reason of insanity. The trial concluded on July 26th, 2006 whereupon Andrea was moved to the North Texas State Hospital, Vernon Campus. Shortly afterwards, she was transferred again, this time to Kerrville State Hospital, a low-security facility in Texas.

Difference of opinion

Rusty had been under a gag order for the entirety of the trial, meaning that he couldn't speak out about his nerves before the verdict. After leaving court it became clear that he had been waiting for this moment for a long time: he told reporters, "It's a miracle." But the prosecution were far from happy with the verdict: "Five years ago, Andrea Yates called police to inform them of what she had done to her five children," prosecutor Joe Owmby told the same group of reporters. "It was no mystery then who ended their lives. We are extremely disappointed with the verdict." The second prosecutor working with Owmby added, "This case has always been about bringing justice for these children," and they felt that justice had not been served in quashing Andrea's sentence.

But Rusty demanded, "Who are they really serving? Do they think the children want Andrea to be in prison? Do they think we, her family on either side, want Andrea to be in prison? Is it of any public benefit for Andrea to be in prison? Is she a danger to anyone?" "It's amazing to me," He went on. "I'm so proud of the jury for seeing past that."

In their explanation for reversing Andrea's conviction, the Court of Appeals judges stated that "there is a reasonable likelihood that Dr. Dietz's false testimony could have affected the judgment of the jury." But Dietz argued the point after the end of the trial: "In short, I made an honest mistake and took immediate action to correct it," he said. "I am angry that a false accusation by a defense lawyer has been so widely promulgated in the press."

The Vice-President of the APA (American Psychiatric Association) spoke extensively to the press in the aftermath of the retrial, expressing her support for the decision. "It is a great relief to hear that justice has prevailed," APA Vice President Nada Stotland, M.D. told Pyshciatric News.

" It's heartbreaking that she was convicted in the first place. It was clear that some people were swayed by their intense feelings about the sanctity of motherhood," she said. "They could not accept any excuse for a mother harming her children. So they thought it was essential that the court send a message that would convince other mothers out there that they couldn't get away with harming their children.

"Others could not grasp the possibility that a person could carry out effective plans and activities while psychotic or on the basis of psychotic beliefs. This is a recurring confusion in cases involving a psychotic defendant.

"There is also a persistent sense that society is too lenient overall, a belief that criminals are claiming insanity far more often than is the case and still far more often than this defense actually prevails. Many people simply don't believe in psychiatric conditions as genuine diseases. They feel that the punishment of those who break the rules is essential to the maintenance of a just society."

That being said, Andrea remained in prison. The fact of her mental illness had not changed, whether she was judged to have been legally sane at the time of the crimes or not. At the very least, she would now be able to receive better treatment for her afflictions than she had in prison- something that both she, and her family, was happy for.

Was it her anti-depressants that were to blame?

Andrea's family, friends and neighbors firmly believe that the anti-depressants she was administered were to blame for her psychotic mental breakdown. According to Suzy Spencer's book about Andrea,

Breaking Point, she was taking 450 mg of Effexor daily, until the final few days before her breakdown, when the amount was drastically reduced by Dr. Saeed. Rusty claimed that he protested to the doctor, since his own research had told him that dramatic reductions in intake of Effexor can have terrible side effects. Nevertheless, Dr. Saeed insisted on lowering the dose.

Dr. Saeed argued that Andrea was already taking far too much of the drug, and that the risks of continuing to take it in such large amounts were greater than the risk of reducing the amount by roughly a third. Homicidal ideation is one of the accepted side-effects of the drug, and Andrea had been taking far too much- twice the recommended dose- for two months prior to the murders. At the trial, Dr. Lucy Puryear gave testimony as an expert witness. She claimed that Dr. Saeed's actions were normal medical practice, and that he could not be held accountable on this front for Andrea's psychotic break. Rather, she claimed, it was the fact that Andrea was taken off her regular dose of Haldol which was to blame.

What about religious influences?

An alternative theory is that Andrea's religious influences were a major cause of the tragedy that occurred. Not long before the event, Rusty met a preacher named Michael Woroniecki: Woroniecki was, and is, well known for his fire and brimstone sermons on the topic of Hell, and for his regular newsletter on the topic of Hell and the Rapture entitled *The Perilous Times*. It was around the time that Rusty met Woroniecki that Andrea's delusions took on the extra dimensions of demonic or satanic possession, prophecy, and references to the end times.

After the trial, ABC Primetime's Chris Cuomo claimed on air: "[Andrea Yates'] delusions were fueled by the extreme religious beliefs of a bizarre, itinerant street preacher named Michael Woroniecki..." He believed that Woroniecki's preaching and writings had inspired Andrea to believe that the end times were coming, and that the devil was at work in her community- and through her children. Woroniecki, of course, denied the accusations. He claimed that he had not been close to the family, a sentiment echoed by Rusty himself.

That being said, it was clear that at some level Andrea's delusions drew upon the ideas of her deeply held religious views. In conversations with her prison psychiatrist, Andrea has since stated that she had long considered killing her children. "It was the seventh deadly sin. My children weren't righteous. They stumbled because I was evil. The way I was raising them, they could never be saved. They were doomed to perish in the fires of hell." Andrea's attorney agreed: "Bottom line [is] she thought she was saving their souls," Parnham told ABC News.

Andrea Yates today

Andrea Yates is, of course, still imprisoned. She is still held at a small mental health facility, Kerrville State Hospital, and will turn 53 this year. Sources close to Yates have told newspapers that she still watches home videos of her young family. Of all the inmates at this particular facility, Yates is the only one not allowed outside. She requested just a two hour pass for permission to go to a nearby church, but this was refused.

Yates herself has refused to talk to the press, but her defense attorney George Parnham has confirmed that she will almost certainly remain at the same facility from now until her death. He has also given a small window into Andrea's life at the hospital, and described his relationship with her. "Long ago, I crossed the professional line," Parnham said. "I treat her as if she were a child of mine."

Describing her everyday life, he said "...There are no wires. There are no fences [at Kerrville]. She wears makeup, wears blue jeans, she wears earrings when she wants to," Parnham said. "She devises little arts and crafts and sells them anonymously at trade shows." Any money she makes is given to the Yates Children Memorial Fund, which was founded by her attorney and his wife Mary. The proceeds go towards women struggling with mental health issues. Despite the changes in her life, Parnham has confirmed that Andrea has few visitors who take the time to see her.

Describing the charity and the effects that it has, Parnham has said "...It turns a tragedy into a positive force. It means a lot to prevent other tragedies in many ways. Now we talk with attorneys about mental health. People always ask me about Andrea in a very compassionate way. That's a far cry from the position the state took years ago, when they sought the death penalty."

Rusty has been asked by the press whether he forgives his wife. "Yes... Forgiveness kind of implies that I have ever really blamed her. In some sense I've never really blamed her because I've always blamed her illness." It has been well over a decade, now, since he and his wife lost their children due to Andrea's mental illness; but no matter the facts of the case, it remains difficult to imagine or sympathise with how Rusty can have forgiven his wife. Most people would not have the strength.

CHILD KILLER MANLING WILLIAMS

82

CRYSTAL STONE

Manling Williams was born in 1979 as Manling Tsang. She tended to go by the nickname "Ling" while growing up. As a child, she was diagnosed with various learning disabilities and experienced many challenges academically while in school. Williams was the result of an unwanted pregnancy between her two parents, and she was nearly aborted. Ultimately, she was born into a family that didn't want her, and they treated her as such throughout her childhood with copious amounts of verbal and physical abuse.

In her childhood, Williams struggled to make friends. At one point when she was growing up, she stole money from her parents in order to buy friends at school, as she couldn't make them no matter how hard she tried. She did not do well socially. That incident resulted in a public scolding that was so severe and inappropriate that Child Protective Services became involved. While her mother was chastising her in front of her peers, she slapped her face repeatedly. Although Child Protective Services was called, nothing tangible came of it, and the case was closed. Manling remained with her parents and her sister for the remainder of her childhood and into her early adulthood.

Many would later testify that Manling's parents repeatedly called her stupid due to her lack of success in school, and that physical abuse went on as well. In one incident, a foreign exchange student who was living with the family recalled that her father slapped her face four or five times when she was suspected of stealing money from a friend. Manling ran to her room in tears.

In 1999, Neal Williams met and fell in love with his 20-year-old coworker at Subway, Manling. "He thought she was beautiful," Neal's mom, Jan Williams, later said in a statement to reporters. "He liked that he could talk to her about a lot of things." Neal was considered to be affable and intelligent. He was well-liked, and liked to watch Star Wars and quote Monty Python. He was considered to be very bright and was particularly close with his mom, Jan, and his older sister, Mala.

Shortly after they began dating, Manling became illegitimately pregnant with Neal's child. On July 26, 2000, Neal and Manling's had a baby boy, whom they named Devon. Devon was described by his grandmother Jan as silly, sociable, and tolerant. He wished to study monkeys when he grew up and attend Whittier College, which is where his grandmother worked. Everyone loved Devon. A family friend had chosen to have him as the ring bearer in her wedding. "He couldn't stand to see someone upset or treated unfairly," the friend recalled. If he saw someone being treated unfairly, or if he saw that someone felt sad or was upset, he took steps to fix it, even at a young age.

Jan Williams recalled one painful memory of Devon having some normal anxiety about nighttime and being afraid of the dark, a memory which stings his grandmother to this day. The two were singing a nighttime song about a dragon. Devon expressed concern because the song alluded to little boys who died in their beds. "I told him he was safe in his bed, and he wasn't," his grandmother later said sadly.

In 2001, Manling and baby Devon were in the car with Judy, Neal's mom. Manling officially asked Judy for permission to marry his son. "Only if you promise not to hurt him," she replied lightly, and the pair laughed, having no idea of knowing what lay ahead.

Having had a child out of wedlock did nothing to improve Williams' ongoing tumultuous relationship with her parents. She was forced to move out of their home and temporarily lived with friends and her mother-in-law, Jan Williams. Neal and Manling eventually became engaged, got married at a courthouse, and later had a big wedding at a Taiwanese church. The trio then moved into a condo in Rowling Heights in Los Angeles county, California, where they would live until everything ended. The neighborhood was cozy and safe, and the neighbors were friendly.

Manling and Neal's second son, Ian, was born in the Fall of 2003. Ian liked to pester his older brother, and "threw himself into life with great abandon," according to his grandmother's recollections. He would do things like get his head stuck between the railings on the banister, build a ladder out of chairs and climb to the top, and knock down whatever structure Devon had just created. He also hated any sort of nickname or pet name, and insisted vehemently, "My name is IAN!"

A few years went by where, by all appearances, Manling, Neal, Devon, and Ian were a happy and regular family. At this time, Williams worked at Marie Callender's as a waitress, while Neal did a lot of computer work from home. In the months leading up to the incident, Manling had connected with an old friend named John Gregory via MySpace, and subsequently began an affair with him. This was a man that she had had an attraction, or rather an infatuation, for since the days of high school. Almost immediately after their affair began, Gregory began to pressure Manling to get a divorce and ended up breaking things off with her shortly after, while promising that they could get back together if she ended up terminating her marriage. Meanwhile, Williams had grown tired of being a mother and a wife, and was feeling very distant from her children.

Beginning in June of 2007, Manling began to randomly tell her friends that she was having dreams of Neal smothering their sons and then killing himself. No one made much of these comments, aside from thinking that they were disturbing and unfortunate. Williams and her husband had been having significant marital problems, often resulting in profanity-laced arguments and slamming doors that could be heard by neighbors outside of their home. The home they lived in was filled with piles of clothes and trash, with unwashed dishes and more trash on the kitchen counters, and was chronically very unkempt. However, despite their marital difficulties, Neal was by all accounts an excellent father. He enjoyed reading to his children, playing catch with them, and taking them to baseball games.

On August 7, 2007, Maling smothered her two young sons with a pillow in their bunk bed, and slashed her husband to death with a sword in the family's condominium. With regard to her children, Ian was in the bottom bunk with a teddy bear blanket, and Devon was in the top bunk, under a Spongebob blanket. Her husband Neal was 27 years old at the time, the same age as Manling. Devon was age seven, and Ian, age three. Autopsy results would show that the boys had died within two hours after eating their last meal, which was pineapple pizza delivered to the home at 8:20 pm. Computer records showed that after she smothered them, Manling left the boys dead in their beds and checked her boyfriend's MySpace page. She then went out with friends to dinner to TGIFridays. A friend who was at dinner with her would later testify that Williams was behaving normally, and that Williams often spoke lovingly of her children. Four days prior to the killings, on August 3, Williams had sent her lover a single red rose, with the message "thinking of you." She had signed it as being from a secret admirer.

Neal was asleep in bed when Mailing returned home. Manling retrieved and used a katana sword that had been given to Neal by his mother, as he was a sword collector. The knife had a 10-inch handle, a 20-inch blade, and was incredibly sharp. While he was sleeping, she stabbed him in the chest. Neal did not die in the bed, which indicated that he had gotten up tried to run in an attempt to escape.

The autopsy report would show that Neal's hands were mangled as he tried to fend off the attack, and he had a giant "X" slashed on his torso. He lost the tips of two fingers and broke several other fingers attempting to defend himself. He had 22 wounds on his hands alone. He only made it as far as the top of the stairs, which was a short distance from their bedroom, and the katana was found near his body. Neal was stabbed and slashed 97 times total in the attack. In his final moments, he begged Williams for help, a call which was left unheeded. He suffered a fatal wound when he was initially stabbed through the heart, damaging his right ventricle and his aorta, which takes blood to the brain. This was actually the first strike from the katana, but it wasn't an immediately fatal one. Autopsy results showed that both of his lungs were punctured and filled with blood (500 cubic centimeters in the right lung, and 200 cubic centimeters in the left). In addition, he suffered a wound through his back that went "through and through" and departed his body via his neck, damaging his thyroid gland in the process. One of the other most damaging wounds went through his small intestine. In addition, a "chopping" type of wound was located on the back of his neck that fractured his skull and caused bleeding in the brain. Neal's mother would end up having chronic, recurrent nightmares of his nearly severed hands after learning about them in trial. Deputy Tim Bryant later testified that he nearly fell when he stepped over Neal, because there was so much blood that had saturated the carpet around him.

Immediately following the murder, Manling typed a fake suicide note on Neal's behalf stating that Neal had killed the children and then himself. The letter stated that Neal was having an affair and hinted at killing the children before committing suicide. "Please for give [sic] me for being a coward and not being there for you," Manling wrote under the guise of Neal's voice. She posted the note on MySpace. She disposed of all bloody clothing in a dumpster a fair distance from their home. These clothes were later recovered and were confirmed to have Neal's blood on them. Then she returned home and ran outside, screaming to neighbors at 7:30 am that someone had killed her family.

Several neighbors ran to assist and after speaking to Manling, went into the house before the police arrived, not understanding what they would find. In court, one neighbor would describe seeing Neal at the top of the stairs. "I seen Neal laying there, stabbed up. I looked into his eyes and blood was just dripping and dripping." This same neighbor found the little boys and described through tears what he found while on the stand. "I shook the little blanket but there was no movement, nothing, no movement."

Manling's account of what had happened became contradictory almost immediately. Upon calling her neighbors over at 7:30 am via her frantic screaming, she told them she had gone out for Red Bull and cigarettes and had returned to find the crime scene. She then told investigators that she had gone for a drive because she couldn't sleep, then later stated that she had gone grocery shopping (though she was wearing boxer shorts, smelled of alcohol, and was barefoot when her neighbors saw her, suggesting that she hadn't recently gone anywhere).

When Neal's mother, Jan Williams, heard the news, she got a ride to the sheriff's station right away, where she met with Manling's parents. The trio hugged and cried as they waited for more news. They waited for Manling to come out after her interview with police. However, Manling was never released, and soon, a terrible realizations began to set in.

For several hours, while being interviewed by investigators following the discovery of the bodies, Manling feigned sadness, grief and bewilderment on camera. She said things like, "Does anyone know if my husband is okay? I want my babies. Please let them be okay." Only after investigators found a bloody cigarette box in her car and confronted her did Williams confess to the crimes. Blood was found in a spot on her bra that matched where Neal's blood was found on the bloody shirt that was thrown into the dumpster. Neal's blood was also found on her feet. After her confession, she was arrested on three counts of homicide one day after the murders, on August 8, 2007.

Detective Donald Walls recalled that Manling was arrogant in her interviews, that she was relaxed as if they were having a normal lunchtime conversation, and that she made jokes about the TV show CSI. The Williams' neighbors in the 18200 block of Camino Bello in Rowland Heights, California, were first shocked and then horrified as police spread crime scene tape around their property and began carrying out multiple bins of evidence. One piece of evidence that was later shown in court was a dictionary that had a page marked by having a knife placed inside. On this page was the definition of the word "marriage." In the yard lay discarded equipment: a football, a bat, and a plastic pitching machine.

Manling originally stated in her confession that Neil had "passed out drunk" the night of the killings, but toxicology reports later showed that he did not have drugs or alcohol in his system. He was sober when he died. After Manling's arrest, it took more than a year for the first preliminary hearing to take place due to repeated delays and postponements. This process was very hard on the victim's family. Neal's mother and sister were particularly open with reporters throughout the process as they waited for the trial process to begin.

With the verdict in, the next part of the legal process was the penalty phase, in which jurors would recommend whether Manling should receive life in prison or the death penalty as her sentence. Manling's defense attorneys, Tom Althaus and Haydeh Takasugi, argued that Manling should receive a life sentence and not the death penalty, arguing that the murders were not calculated, but rather "a sudden mistake," and that Manling was in a state of "extreme emotional and mental disturbance" when the killings occurred. They noted that "it was clear that the family unit was unraveling." However, as Los Angeles County Deputy District Attorneys Stacy Okun-Wiese and Pak Kouch pointed out, Williams had put on latex gloves prior to killing her husband, indicating that the killing could not be correctly defined as "spur of the moment." The defense attempted to paint Manling as a socially awkward loner who was mentally unstable and who was overburdened by cultural expectations.

The defense also argued that Williams had a difficult upbringing, and that her life was defined by pain, heartbreak, and "diminished dreams." They noted that she was reputed to be a very charitable person prior to the killings, that she was previously well known for lovin her husband and children (a contradictory assertion to several neighborhood eyewitnesses), and that she had no history of violence. A few additional witnesses continued to contradict this picture, however, such as one of her neighbors, who indicated that Manling rarely said more than hello, and that "she would just stand outside her house, smoking and smoking." The defense focused almost solely on the upbringing and abuse Williams experienced at the hands of her mother. Manling's father, Kai Tai Tsang, while on the stand, appealed directly to Neal's mother and apologized. "I feel really sorry. Please forgive me. As a father, I didn't do good. That is why it happened. I am sorry."

Williams' former lover, John Gregory, testified that after Manling contacted him on MySpace in June of 2007, the two went to dinner with two other people from their high school, during which time Manling discussed that she wasn't happy at home or in her relationship. In July of 2007, Manling went to see Gregory in Santa Barbara for a weekend, and the two had an affair. According to his testimony, Gregory ended the affair a few days later. He reported that Manling seemed "normal" throughout the affair and also upon breaking up. Gregory had initially denied the affair to investigators, but later came clean. "I felt really uncomfortable and slightly responsible that I contributed to her emotional state," he said. Manling's friend Melaney Ramirez also testified with regard to Williams' emotional state, saying that according to previous conversations they had had, Manling felt forced into marriage because she accidentally became pregnant. Another friend, Jaclyn Bailey, testified that Manling and Neal would fight "almost every day," and that the fights would often escalate to screaming. Bailey also stated that she had lived with the Williams for three months, and that she was "beyond shocked" because she always thought Williams loved her children, even if there were struggles in the marriage.

With regard to whether or not the killings were premeditated, testimony during Williams' trial indicated that the suffocation method of using a pillow by which she killed her first child took five to 10 minutes, which was ample time for Williams to consider her actions. However, she then went on to kill her second child in precisely the same way. This in additional to wearing the latex gloves and mentioning the manner of death to friends up to two months prior to the killings, made it difficult for the defense to form a solid argument about the killings being spur of the moment.

Neal's mother was present during the trial and was often seen taking notes on what was being presented in an almost clinical manner. However, one week into the trial, she broke down as blood spatter pictures were being shown to the jury, and she saw one of her grandson's favorite stuffed animals (a dragon that her grandsons had named Puff) in the background of the photo. She was also forced to watch a clip of Manling calmly telling a detective what Neal's last words were ("Help me").

Mangling went to trial in November of 2010, and the trial took approximately six weeks. A jury, after deliberating for eight hours, convicted Manling of three counts of first-degree murder, along with the special allegations of using weapons and lying in wait. The jury of six men and six women was unable to agree, with a vote of 8-4, on whether life in prison or the death penalty was a more appropriate punishment, so the decision was given to a second jury. The second jury recommended in 2011 that Williams be put to death.

There was much controversy around the sequence of the two juries who were tasked with deciding the outcome for Williams. Manling's sister, Shun Ling Tsang, urged the judge to consider life without parole instead of the death penalty rather than retrying the penalty phase after the first hung jury. She had given testimony during the trial that her sister's behavior had changed in the months leading up to the murders, and that she would often call her sister in the middle of the night "just to talk," which was new and unusual behavior. She argued that the prosecution's continued pursuit of the death penalty was "ego driven" and "politically motivated." After the first jury was unable to come to a decision, members of both families asserted that they would prefer to see a life sentence with no possibility of parole, and no possibility of appeal. The defense again appealed for life in prison over the death penalty, emphasizing Manling's lack of previous violence, as well as her difficult upbringing. However, the prosecution decided to re-try the penalty phase, which resulted in the death penalty. The second penalty phase of the trial began on April 18, 2011. Prosecuting attorney Stacy Okun-Wiese scoffed at the defense's attempt to pin the murders on Manling's childhood, stating "When did it become okay in our society to commit three heinous crimes, kill your children and your husband, and blame it on your mom?"

Williams was sentenced to death on January 8, 2012 for the murders of her family per the jury's recommendation. "It is the order of the court that you should suffer the penalty of death," Judge Robert Martinez said to Manling. She was 32 years old at the time of her sentencing. Manling, dressed in an orange prison jumper with glasses on, sat in handcuffs and stared down at the table during the duration of the sentencing, then sobbed and visibly shook after the support was read. She leaned on her defense attorney, Haydeh Takasugi, who openly cared about Williams on a personal level, and who was deeply invested in the case. Manling was often seen in court that way - head down, eyes down, unable to look the world in the face.

Neal's mother, Jan Williams, expressed gratitude that the trial was finally over, citing the "terrible" impact the events had had on everyone involved, including the Tsang family. She has stated "This is their tragedy, too. I don't blame them for anything." It had been very difficult for her to attend as many hearings and trial events as she had over the past four years, but she made herself go until resolution of the case.

She felt that it was her responsibility to be present at every court date because someone had to be there to "represent the victims."

Pomona Superior Court Judge Robert Martinez stated "The evidence is compelling that the defendant, for selfish reasons, murdered her own two children." He called her desire to start a new life with another man "narcissistic, selfish, and adolescent." He noted that Williams had many family members who would have willingly taken the boys in, and that their deaths were abhorrently unnecessary. He remarked that each of the three killings was deliberate and premeditated without question. Lastly, he remarked that he was not in the position to forgive, as "the ones in the position to forgive are not with us."

There is some question as to whether or not Williams will actually ever undergo execution. California is known for delaying executions for those on death row indefinitely. There are over 700 people who have been sentenced to death in California. However, only 13 people have put to death in California since 1976, none of whom have been the other 19 women who are already on death row in California. Neal's mother took some comfort in the resolution of the case. "The legal process will no doubt go on for probably the rest of my lifetime. But I feel like I am leaving something behind today. Something is finished," she told reporters.

One of the most notable things about Manling has been her silence. She has essentially gone radio silent since her incarceration. She has reportedly become involved with the church services within the prison where she resides, and the leader of this church testified in court that she had come to know Manling well and that she didn't feel she was "evil." It was also shared in court that many of the children who knew Devon and Ian became very traumatized upon learning of their deaths, and even more so when they learned that they were killed by their own mother.

Jan Williams maintains a blog to this day that is open to the public and started almost immediately after the death, detailing her memories, events, and coping with regard to what happened to her family. It's called Grief's Journey, and provides a raw and rare insight into the life of a survivor of a murder victim. She also keeps a fairly public Facebook page, which shows a morbid and personal look into her experience over the course of the trial. In a post from 2010, Jan writes, "In planning a suicide, it might be well to remember that it is very difficult to stab yourself repeatedly in the back, especially when your hands and fingers have been severed. That's free advice."

CHILD KILLER PAULINE ZILE

CRYSTAL DENNIS

Pauline Zile was born June 13, 1970 as Pauline Yingling. Some reports assert that her mother, Paula Yingling, abandoned Pauline in her childhood. However, her mother was a visible presence later in Pauline's life and the two now appear to be close. Pauline's father, conversely, is little more than a question mark. Pauline's only sibling, Matt Yingling, grew up to be a firefighter and emergency technician, and John Yingling, their only other known immediate relative, is Pauline's maternal grandfather. The two were not close, and John was very removed from the events of her life.

While many facets of Pauline's early childhood remain unknown, we do know that she had a difficult adolescence. When Pauline would undergo a murder trial for the death of her daughter as a young adult, her defense team was notably silent on her upbringing and provided few, if any, facts about who she was or where she came from.

We do know that as a teenager and then as a young adult, Pauline moved from one ramshackle apartment to the next, and had little in the way of education. She became pregnant while dating a teenage boy named Frank Holt in 10th grade at age 16, and subsequently dropped out of high school.

This pregnancy resulted in marriage, and their child, Christina Diane Holt, was born five months later on May 23, 1987. Being a married teenage mother proved to be too difficult for Pauline, and the marriage resulted in divorce not long after it began, one year later. Frank Holt filed for divorce on June 14, 1988, and initially expressed interest in gaining custody of Christina, as he stated that Pauline was an unfit mother who was also a flight risk. Around this time, she began taking part in a series of jobs in different restaurants. According to Maryland court records, she also struggled with drug and alcohol issues, as did Christina's father. Christina never lived with her father in her short life.

Pregnancy would remain a major theme of Pauline's teenage and early adulthood years. By the age of 24, she had become pregnant and borne children three additional times. However, Pauline gave her first child Christina up willingly as she was only 17 when Christina was born, and her marriage had failed. "It was a case of babies trying to raise babies," her mother later said to a newspaper in an interview.

Christina went to live with her paternal step-great-grandmother, Dorothy Money, as neither parent showed any serious interest in permanent custody and both continued to struggle with drugs and alcohol. Christina would live with Dorothy from the age of five months to five years. They lived in a comfortable, middle-class neighborhood in Maryland. Christina was reported by friends and neighbors as a sweet girl who was very outgoing. Money reported that Pauline would come up from her residence in Florida to see Christina once per year, but also stated that their visits were short, and that neither Christina nor her mother seemed to feel very comfortable or enjoy their visits very much, particularly in Christina's younger years. When Christina was five, Dorothy signed guardianship over to her adopted daughter, Judy Holt, who lived a block and a half away. Dorothy struggled with severe arthritis and was 70 years old. Christina would still come to spend weekends with her, and Dorothy kept her room with her pink canopy bed just the way it was in anticipation of her visits.

Judy Holt kept Christina for 22 months, but eventually decided that she did not wish to raise Christina long-term, and felt that Christina should be raised by her mother. By all accounts, Christina was very excited to live in Florida with her mother, and to meet the two little half-brothers that she had heard of but never seen. It has been reported that Judy Holt drove Christina to Florida with little to no notice to Pauline and left her in her care. It was this lack of notice that was likely the first in a series of events that led to Christina's death. Dorothy Money later reported that Judy had taken Christina to Florida without her knowledge, and she was so upset about this fact that she severed the relationship with her adopted daughter. Dorothy did not know Pauline's phone number, and she never spoke to Christina or Pauline again.

When Christina was two years old, Pauline met and married John Zile at age 19, who had moved to Florida in 1987, violating his probation. She quickly bore him two sons, and stated later that John forced her to get an abortion for an additional pregnancy. When Christina was unexpectedly left in their care, she was seven months pregnant with an additional baby that she would later give up for adoption due to financial issues. When Zile went back to Maryland to face charges that he had violated his probation, Pauline wrote a letter to the judge pleading for his release, and describing how she was having difficulty paying rent without him, even while working two jobs. In the letter, she described him as a "terrific guy."

John Zile had a troubled youth. Records show that he spent part of his youth incarcerated on unspecified charges in three different involuntary youth shelters and one group home. He had a ninth-grade education and had once been suspended for "being rowdy," according to school records from 1986. In 1984, he was found guilty of burglary, as he had broken into a home and stolen a rifle and some silverware. He was given a five-year sentence, broke probation twice, and served several additional months as a result. He was described as having drug and alcohol problems and bouncing among odd jobs (such as painting cars, working in restaurants, and installing drywall) and lived in a series of different residences throughout his life.

Pauline continued to lead a difficult existence with her husband and children, often having to live in pay-by-the-week motel rooms in order to get by. Neighbors reported that she was at one time going door-to-door and selling children's videotapes in order to obtain gas money. A former landlord of the Ziles stated, "I felt sorry for them. I don't know why. Her eyes always looked sad, truthfully. I just thought maybe it was from working all the time and being with the kids when she was off work; she never had time for herself." The same landlord also reported that Pauline worked hard while John drifted from job to job, staying inside all day, blasting music late at night, and often quitting his short-term jobs without notice.

One neighbor said Pauline and John's two young boys were often spotted in the windowsills of their apartment, banging on the windows and waving at anyone who passed. They would continue this behavior until their father saw them and pulled them away from the windows. The Ziles would not allow management into their apartment for cleaning or repairs. Neighbors reported that Pauline didn't even let the children out to play, and they would forego invitations to birthday parties and playdates. The Ziles worked a succession of restaurant jobs after meeting one another, often together (he as a cook, and she as a waitress). Their landlord later reported that Pauline and the children rarely left the apartment, and that John always answered the door, and he always delivered the rent money.

The landlord who managed the complex had a son who noted that that conditions in the residence were horrible. "It was dirty. When you'd walk by the room and the door was open, there was stuff all over the floor. The kids' room was really dirty and it smelled. There were clothes everywhere, food on the tables, potato chips and shoes, toys, glasses, paper cups and stuff."

Sometimes after work, Pauline would want to get a drink with her coworkers. However, one of these colleagues later reported that John would call her and tell her to get home and take care of the kids. One neighbor reported that Pauline and John didn't get along well, and that she would often go days at a time without hearing from him. Prior to her sudden and expected arrival, Pauline spoke fondly of Christina to these colleagues. She would show them pictures, talked about how well she was doing in school, and talked about how they would exchange packages and cards through the mail. Pauline also stated to her neighbor, Donna Dunn, that she left Christina in

Maryland because she couldn't afford to give her a good life, but that she hoped they would be reunited and live together someday.

After having lived with relatives in Maryland for most of her live, she moved in with her mother, her stepfather, and her two younger half-brothers in a one-bedroom apartment in Riviera Beach. Four months later, she was dead. It wasn't long after her unexpected arrival that the abuse at the hands of her stepfather began. At one point, John beat Christina in a bedroom in front of a family friend named Chad Brannon. He picked her up by the shirt, threw her on the bed, beat her repeatedly with a belt, and then pulled down her pants and showed Chad the welts caused by the injuries, according to information provided by Chad during testimony.

Christina was kept out of school in the weeks leading up to her murder in order to hide her frequent injuries. She had only attended school for a total of five out of 22 days that year. Her murder took place on September 16, 1994. Christina was in second grade. She was three feet, nine inches tall, and weighed 44 pounds. Her death occurred around midnight. She was beaten to death by her stepfather, John Zile, while Pauline stood by and watched, failing to intervene. Christina was beaten until she collapsed and went into convulsions, and was found to have ultimately died by suffocation as she choked on her own blood and vomit. John Zile had held his hand over her mouth and also stuffed a towel in her mouth during the beating to muffle the sound of her screams and cries. John Zile later admitted that the girl was beaten after repeatedly soiling herself and defecating on the floor, but called the death an accident.

The Ziles' former next-door neighbor, Dayle Ackerman, testified that she had overheard the murder. She was getting dressed when she heard a man say "Why did you shit on the floor in front of me?" The neighbor then heard the sounds of the shouting, crying, and hitting. She later testified that heard the man hitting the screaming child over and over until the child fell silent. She did not do anything to assist the child or to intervene. Ackerman testified that she then heard a female voice say, "John, that's enough." In her final moments, Ackerman did not hear Christina calling for her mother. Prior to the fatal beating, neighbors reported that they heard John cursing at and slapping the girl on multiple occasions. After the beating, John Zile reported that he tried to revive Christina via CPR and by dunking her in a tub of cold water, but it was too late.

Pauline was eight months pregnant at the time, and ended up having her fourth child from prison shortly thereafter, who was given up for adoption immediately afterward. Three days later, she went to Christina's elementary school and withdrew her, but did not ask for any school records. This was unusual as school records are often required for enrollment in another school. As they days and weeks went by, Pauline tried to hide the death by telling school officials that Christina had returned to her home in Maryland. She pawned her daughter's bicycle and videotapes, and used that money to purchase the shovel and tarp to bury her daughter. John buried a five and a half foot grave, then threw that shovel over a bridge.

Four weeks after Christina's death, Pauline went on television to plead tearfully for the return of her daughter, suggesting that she had been kidnapped from the restroom of a flea market in Fort Lauderdale called the Swap Shop. During this television appearance, Pauline pleaded for her return, but also kept referring to Christina in the past tense ("She was a nice girl"). She also led authorities to her car, where she had planted a half-empty bottle of juice and a half-eaten bag of candy on the car seat. She concocted a story about how she and Christina had planned to spend the day at the beach. Pauline described specific details about her fictional trip to the Swap Shop with Christina, stating that Christina was excited about seeing the circus and going on the amusement rides.

As a result of Pauline's appearance on television, Christina's photo was plastered across local and state news media, which prompted a frantic search and also generated a lot of public interest and concern in this particular case. Over 10,000 flyers were posted throughout southern Florida by the Adam Walsh Center, who became involved in the case. The Ziles and Christina's biological father taped separate interviews about the case for America's Most Wanted. This public interest and concern carried would carry over into the subsequent trials of her parents.

Police became suspicious soon after Pauline's missing child report. There were no witnesses that reported ever seeing Christina at the Swap Shop. Authorities discovered that she had been withdrawn from school several weeks earlier, but not placed in a new one. They also discovered that no one had seen Christina alive in quite some time. They obtained a search warrant and examined the Zile's residence. Blood was found throughout the apartment, including on a pair of Christina's jeans, her bed, the walls, and the floor. Traces were also found in the couple's car and on some knives in a toolbox that was in the trunk. The couple had kept Christina's body wrapped in blankets and sheets in a closet for several days before burying her. She was buried in a vacant lot near a shopping center in Tequesta, Florida. In the separate trials for both parents, the coroner would report that Christina had bruises on her left eyebrow, left lower jaw, left cheek ,and right cheek. Bruises were also found on both arms, her right leg, her right knee, her thigh, and on her buttocks. There was a deep cut inside her mouth that occurred due to the blunt force trauma she experienced.

John's boss later commented that he worked side-by-side with John in the days following her murder. "I saw no signs of emotion, no signs of stress. It just blows my mind," he stated. The woman who lived next door to the Ziles, Linda Kauppinen, said that the knowledge of Christina's death haunted her daily. "Every time I closed my eyes, I saw her in that closet." The back of Linda's closet touched the back of the Ziles' closet where Christina was temporarily kept. "I just kept getting that picture."

Pauline's two youngest children told investigators that John beat Christina's buttocks, that Pauline and John did not like Christina, and that Christina was dead. During the early stages of the investigation, the Ziles continued to arouse suspicion by halfheartedly fleeing from authorities and not showing up for requested appointments with police. In one instance, Christina was reported found (which was obviously an error). Pauline did not rush to see the child, which investigators found to be odd. The Ziles spent some time during the investigation staying with Pauline's mother. In late October 1994, as the investigation grew more heated, the couple tried and failed at a double-suicide in an orange grove. They had planned to asphyxiate themselves in their white Cadillac. Eventually, after failing a lie detector test and being interrogated for several hours, Pauline came clean and implicated her husband in the killing in exchange for limited immunity. After hearing that his wife had made a statement, John decided to "come clean," to "do the right thing," and he led authorities to Christina's grave.

One wonders how much Paula Yingling knew about Christina's case, given some of the oddly specific quotes she gave in the early days of the search for Christina, who was initially considered missing. "We're just very, very upset and are hoping for her safe return. From what I'm told, police don't think anyone in the family had anything to do with this,"

After John's arrest, authorities worked to determine if they had cause to charge Pauline as well, given that she had limited immunity for the statement she had made to police. During this time, she continued to stay at her mother's beach house, where she received frequent death threats from the public.

Eventually Pauline was charged with first-degree murder, a charge that matched John's. Both were potentially eligible for the death penalty. Prior to her trial, Pauline released a statement through her attorney, saying "I pray that everyone who ever knew and will know me will forgive me for not being a strong person and eventually will trust me again. I will never forget seeing Christina on the living room floor nor her laying on the bed."

During Pauline's trial, it was noted by many that a primary goal of the defense was to make Pauline look as youthful and innocent as possible by dressing her in all pastels, and making her look like little more than a child herself. This wasn't a difficult task, as the brown-haired, blue-eyed woman in her early twenties stood at a little over five foot three.The defense team, which was a well-known father-son attorney duo, argued that Pauline was dominated by her husband, and that she was both helpless and powerless to stop the beatings against Christina. They even asserted that she was "as much a victim as Christina herself." A friend of Christina's described her on the stand as a "weak female," and said it was difficult for her to go against the grain, even if it included or resulted in the death of her daughter.

A witness from The Swap Shop said he saw Pauline rehearsing her television appearance, and was doing what she could in that rehearsal to appear frantic. Neither Pauline nor Christina showed up on the security tapes at the Swap Shop.

Ninety minutes after closing arguments, Pauline was found guilty of first-degree murder and was sentenced to life in prison without possibility of parole on June 7, 1995. She was 24 years old. She was also convicted of three counts of aggravated child abuse, each carrying a sentence of 13 years, to be served concurrently with her life sentence. Upon being sentenced, Pauline remarked, "At least I can sleep tonight," through tears as she was ushered away. As part of the sentencing, she was also forced to give up her remaining two children (Chad, age three, and Daniel, age five at the time). The two boys were adopted together by an unknown family. Pauline has stated that the family does keep her updated on their lives.

The judge remarked that the evidence showed that Pauline was unhappy when Judy Holt brought Christina to live with her, and that she viewed Christina as an unnecessary expense. He also acknowledged that this incident was the first time she had technically been charged with a crime, despite her previous drug and alcohol issues, and noted that he saw her risk as a future danger to society as minimal. This was his rationale as to why she was sentenced to life in prison rather than given the death penalty.

In May of 1994, John Zile's first trial began and ended in a mistrial because the jury was deadlocked. 11 of the jurors felt the charge of first degree murder was an adequate punishment, but one lone juror disagreed, held out for second-degree murder, and would not budge. The second trial had to be dismissed because the judge decided that a court clerk's comments had contaminated potential jurors. The third trial, however, reached its conclusion without incident.

In December of 1996, John Zile was sentenced to life in prison without the possibility of parole for Christina's murder. He also received an additional 30 year sentence for being found guilty on three counts of aggravated child abuse. The defense argued that John never meant to kill Christina, and that his actions after her death "shouldn't be considered."

In October of 1999, the Florida Supreme Court dismissed an appeal Pauline had filed that argued that the statement she gave to police to implicate her husband ended up being used against her as well, and violated her constitutional rights. Six years after Christina's murder, Pauline gave her first interview from the maximum-security prison where she is still held.She described a "pain that's always there," and said she often thinks about what she should or could have done in retrospect. She also stated that she still loves John Zile, though she's not "in love" with him. She argued that she isn't guilty of murder, and said her defense team's representation was grossly inadequate and resulted in the loss of the case. "I don't deserve to be here," she said. "I know I did wrong, but I don't think it's right for me to sit here for the rest of my life for a crime I didn't commit."

Pauline has learned to express her wants and needs in prison, according to jail records. She has requested a mirror to maintain her appearance, a roommate to assuage loneliness, and has also sought education to obtain her high school diploma. She specifically requested to room with Clover Boykin, a notorious woman accused of killing her five-month-old baby, as well as a nine-month-old baby that she had babysat. In a letter written to jail officials, she wrote, "The protective custody lockdown for my own safety does not affect me. It's the long, lonely days and nights I don't like." Pauline was separated from other inmates, who considered mothers who murdered (or took part in murdering) their children to be "the snake's belly" of the prison population and they were targets for acts of violence. Other inmates also wrote letters and started petitions stating that Zile was receiving special treatment, and that certain deputies "treated her like a celebrity."

During this time, she also filed an additional motion in Palm Beach Circuit Court to have her conviction overturned, and was representing herself.

The Zile case set a number of legal precedents. Her conviction of first degree murder due to failure to protect her child was the first of its type in the nation. She was also the first woman to be sentenced to first-degree murder following a new Florida state law that removed the possibility of parole for those who were found guilty of this crime.

There was much public interest in this case, and the area where Christina's grave was marked was a shrine of sorts for quite some time, with a large cross, notes to Christina, and a variety of stuffed animals left by wellwishers and those who wished that something could have been done to save Christina before it was too late.

It has been noted that gender played a role in this case, specifically with differential application of the criminal law codes. Around the time of Christina's death, a little boy in Florida who was living with his father and stepmother was killed by his stepmother after repeated abuse. Unlike Pauline Zile, a first degree murder charge was not brought against the father for "failing to protect his child," and he was "allowed to get on with his life after the tragedy of losing his son." Some critics have argued that Pauline received a harsher sentence because she is female and the parenting standards and expectations are not applied in a uniform way.

Pauline Zile is now 46 years old. The public still doesn't really know who she is. Two pictures have been painted of her: One is that of an irresponsible and manipulative woman, who chose her husband over her child, and who coldly faked a missing child story for police and television cameras. The other picture is that of an insecure and weak woman, a high school dropout, who once pleaded with a judge to release the man she loved. In all likelihood, she is a combination of the two. Whoever she is, she will remain in prison for the remainder of her days. We may never know her true feelings regarding the death of her daughter, or whether she ever did feel any genuine regret or remorse for what happened to Christina.